PRESENTING THE ANTICHRIST
AND FALSE PROPHET

Warning to Jerusalem

CRAIG C. WHITE

Jesus: Thank you for your forgiveness and for the illumination to understand the things that are written in your book so that I might be able to write this book.

Yours, Craig C. White

Turkish President Recep Tayyip Erdogan wants to invade Syria very soon. This is very big news. For those of you who read my books you already know that the Bible describes an attack on Syria and its capital city of Damascus that comes from the Turkish border. Word of this attack will first be heard in the northwest Syrian cities of Hamah and Aleppo. Then the residents of Damascus will flee to Jordan and Damascus will be destroyed.

Destroying Damascus is something that the Antichrist will do!

Contents

PRESENTING THE ANTICHRIST
AND FALSE PROPHET

Copyright 2015 Craig C. White

Preface   **page 9**
Erdogan and Gulen

Chapter One   **page 11**
Obama is NOT the Antichrist!

Chapter Two   **page 17**
Alexis Tsipras is NOT the Antichrist!

Chapter Three   **page 21**
Saudi Prince Alwaleed bin Talal is NOT the Antichrist

Chapter Four   **page 23**
Erdogan is the Antichrist!

Chapter Five   **page 29**
Antichrist checklist

Chapter Six   page 35
Leopard map update!

Chapter Seven   page 39
The little horn is a big pain

Chapter Eight   page 41
Does the Antichrist know that he is the son of perdition?

Chapter Nine   page 47
Revelation 13 – Image of the beast

Chapter Ten   page 59
Revelation 13 Wounded

Chapter Eleven   page 61
Obama is supporting Erdogan

Chapter Twelve   page 63
Intelligence reports reach Hamath

Chapter Thirteen   page 65
Aiming for Hamah

Chapter Fourteen   page 69
Hamah and Aleppo (and Arpad)

Chapter Fifteen   page 75
Antichrist identified?!

Chapter Sixteen   page 81
SPOILER ALERT! Erdogan is the Antichrist!

Chapter Seventeen   page 85
Elkosh O'gosh!

Chapter Eighteen   page 87
Mosul weather forecast

Chapter Nineteen   page 89
ISIS just 10 miles from Nahum tomb!

Chapter Twenty   page 91
Revealing the Antichrist & False Prophet

Chapter Twenty One   page 95
Closing prep schools in Turkey

Chapter Twenty Two   page 97
Turkey-Israeli reconciliation agreement

Chapter Twenty Three   page 99
Obadiah

Chapter Twenty Four   page 103
Turkey Parliament election results

Chapter Twenty Five   page 105
Will Erdogan reconcile with Gulen?

Chapter Twenty Six   page 109
AKP and Republican People's Party coalition a possibility

Chapter Twenty Seven   page 111
Gulen is the man of the hour

Chapter Twenty Eight   page 113
Egypt's Evil President Morsi will be reinstated!

Chapter Twenty Nine   page 117
Tribulation checklist

Chapter Thirty   page 123
WARNING TO JERUSALEM

About the Author   page 127
Craig C. White

www.hightimetoawake.com

More from High Time to Awake

Available from Amazon.com, CreateSpace.com, and other retail outlets. Also available on Kindle and other devices.

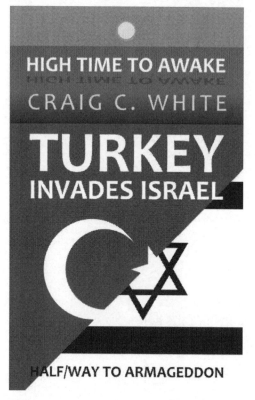

Turkey invades Israel - Halfway to Armageddon alerts us to a coming invasion into Israel led by Turkey! It is called the battle of Gog and Magog in Ezekiel chapter 38. You probably don't realize that you need to know all there is about the battle of Gog and Magog, but trust me this subject is about to define our time in biblical history! The Turkish led battle of *Gog and Magog* is the fulfillment of **the preeminent** pre-Tribulation bible prophecy!

www.hightimetoawake.com

Preface

Erdogan and Gulen

Presenting the Antichrist and False Prophet

By Craig C. White

Turkish President Erdogan and his AKP Party had hopes of gaining a two thirds majority in the Turkish Parliament. The AKP party won 41% of the vote. Some say that President Erdogan lost some of his influence in Turkey's June 7th, 2015 election. But Erdogan's AKP party won the parliamentary elections by a large percentage so I wouldn't say that he was out of power. He has been presented with some obstacles though. His party is faced with forming a coalition government with another party.

It seems that Erdogan won't let this slow him down. He has responded violently to the election results. He has arrested a newspaper editor, and has also arrested several government officials suspected of being part of the Gulen movement. Turkish Muslim cleric Fethullah Gulen is Erdogan's chief rival for political influence in Turkey. Erdogan is also suspected of staging terrorist attacks in Turkey so he can blame them on Gulen and on the Republican People's Party which is the major opposition party.

I suspect that Erdogan will eventually reconcile with Imam Fethullah Gulen and form a coalition party with the Republican People's Party. Gulen is the perfect figure to fulfill the role of False Prophet. He teaches a brand of Islam that includes other faiths. But don't be fooled. Fethullah Gulen is an Islamist at heart.

Erdogan finally called on the AKP party to form a coalition government in early July 2015. As president, Erdogan can call for another election if no coalition is formed within 45 days. If Erdogan does call for another election, then his party risks losing even more seats in the Parliament.

President Erdogan has also responded violently to the election results by beginning an assault on Syria before a coalition government can be formed. According to the bible the Antichrist will invade Syria and then invade Israel just like the ancient Assyrian kings did.

I am certain that Erdogan will attack Syria and destroy Damascus (Jeremiah 49). I am even more certain that he will lead Libya, Iran, and Sudan into Israel (Ezekiel 38).

When Erdogan conquers Syria then the entire Muslim world will hail him as the promised Sultan of a new Islamic World Empire. Muslim cleric Fethullah Gulen's role will be to convince the world to follow Erdogan.

Erdogan is the Antichrist and Fethullah Gulen is the False Prophet.

Chapter One

Obama is NOT the Antichrist!

Photo credit: Michael Verdi www.flickr.com

The Antichrist is a prince

Daniel 7:8

By Craig C. White

US President Barack Obama is not the Antichrist, although he may play a role in end time bible prophecy. In the bible the Antichrist is not identified as a President or king or primary ruler. The Antichrist is identified as a secondary ruler that will ultimately become the head of the final gentile World Empire. US President Obama was a senator for a short time but he is best identified in his role in world politics as a king or president.

Dan 9:26 And after threescore and two weeks shall Messiah be cut off, but not for himself: and the people of the prince that shall come shall destroy the city and

the sanctuary; and the end thereof *shall be* with a flood, and unto the end of the war desolations are determined.

The Antichrist is primarily a prince or secondary ruler. He will become king of the next World Empire; otherwise known as the "New World Order". The New World Order is a world government that probably covers the same territories as the ancient World Empires covered; namely from Europe to India. So the US may not be part of the next World Empire.

The Antichrist is called a "little horn" in Daniel 7:8.

Dan 7:8 I considered the horns, and, behold, there came up among them another little horn, before whom there were three of the first horns plucked up by the roots: and, behold, in this horn *were* eyes like the eyes of man, and a mouth speaking great things.

Horns commonly represent kings in bible prophecy. The *"little horn"* is a secondary ruler, for instance a prince, vice-president, or governor. The term *"little horn"* is applied to Antiochus Epiphanies in Daniel 8:9.

Dan 8:9 And out of one of them came forth a little horn, which waxed exceeding great, toward the south, and toward the east, and toward the pleasant *land*.

Antiochus Epiphanies was the son of "Antiochus the Great" the king of the Seleucid Dynasty. The Seleucid Dynasty ruled over one quarter of the Grecian Empire. The Seleucid Dynasty was headquartered in Antioch of Syria which is now part of Turkey. Antiochus Epiphanies was initially a prince in the Seleucid Dynasty until he manipulated his way onto the throne. The *"little horn"* in Daniel chapter 7 will evidently take away or usurp the authority of three of the first ten kings that rule over the next World Empire. This *"little horn"* has a *"mouth speaking great things"*. He blasphemes God, *"showing himself that he is God"* (Daniel 11:36-37). This little horn is obviously the Antichrist (1

John 2:18). By the way, the Antichrist will do many of the same things that Antiochus Epiphanies did. He will conquer Egypt and ransack Jerusalem. The Antichrist will stop temple sacrifices in Jerusalem just like Antiochus Epiphanies did in 167 BC.

Jesus returns to the earth in fury at the end of Jerusalem's *Great Tribulation*. He dismantles the next World Empire and tosses the Antichrist into the "lake of fire". The Antichrist will be the first resident of the "lake of fire", along with the "False Prophet".

Daniel chapter 7 describes four kings that combine their kingdoms together to create the next World Empire. The first kingdom is represented by a lion with eagle's wings. I think that this lion with eagle's wings represents England since a lion with eagle's wings is actually on their national crest. In the verse below, the eagle wings were plucked off. The eagle is the symbol of the United States. In 1776 the United States (eagle) separated from England (lion). I'm not sure but the eagle wings in Daniel 7:4 may indicate that the United States will assist England in the formation of the next World Empire.

Dan 7:4 The first was like a lion, and had eagle's wings: I beheld till the wings thereof were plucked, and it was lifted up from the earth, and made stand upon the feet as a man, and a man's heart was given to it.

A US leader may participate in the creation of the final gentile World Empire or "New World Order" but probably as an adjunct member. This US leader may be President Barack Obama or perhaps Obama will play a different role. It may be that Barack Obama will be one of four primary "Kings" that create the "New World Order" but perhaps not as a US President!

Turkish President Erdogan is endeavoring to create a new Islamic Union! That is why he wants to invade Syria and remove Syrian President Assad from power. The first four nations to join this new Islamic Union are likely to be Turkey, Syria, Iraq, and Iran (notice that the leopard in Dan 7:6 has four heads). This may be the leopard described in Daniel chapter 7.

Dan 7:6 After this I beheld, and lo another, like a leopard, which had upon the back of it four wings of a fowl; the beast had also four heads; and dominion was given to it.

Current world events regarding this verse compelled me to write my commentary titled "The Leopard is Upon Us!" I believe that the confederacy of nations represented by a leopard in Daniel 7:6 is about to be formed. According to my interpretation, the beasts in Daniel 7 represent coalitions of nations and empires. Currently no nations are symbolized by the leopard. However in November 2014 Turkish President Erdogan announced his intentions to form a new Islamic Union. This Islamic Union could be symbolized by the leopard.

Barack Obama has described Turkish President Erdogan as the US's "most trusted ally". Barack Obama and Turkish President Erdogan are very close friends. I am not predicting this and there is no biblical evidence to support this theory; but Barack Obama may participate in this new Islamic Union in some way. This is just a wild guess but Barack Obama could even become the king over the new Islamic Union.

Barack Obama is also spearheading an effort to form a confederacy of four nations: Pakistan, India, Afghanistan, and Turkmenistan (please note that the leopard also has four wings). There are several reasons for doing this, not the least of which is that Turkmenistan wants to build the world's largest natural gas pipeline to the Arabian Sea. The beginnings of this confederacy already exist. It is called TAPI (Turkmenistan, Afghanistan, Pakistan, and India). This confederacy centers on The Trans-Afghanistan Pipeline.

If you will remember that former Pakistani President Pervez Musharraf was served an arrest warrant for the Benazir Bhutto assassination. Musharraf fled Pakistan and was exile in London and Dubai. He was never tried. He is now back in Pakistan. Well former Pakistani President Pervez Musharraf has gleefully expressed his desire to have US president Barrack Obama as their "Supreme Leader".

Perhaps Barrack Obama will become ruler over these TAPI nations. Maybe he will become king over the leopard? Or perhaps he will just retire to Hawaii.

The Antichrist is primarily identifiable as a prince or secondary ruler. US President Barrack Obama is best identified as a king or primary ruler. Barack Obama is not the Antichrist but that doesn't mean that he won't play a role in end time bible prophecy.

By the way newly elected Turkish President Erdogan has been President of Turkey for just six months. On the other hand Erdogan served as Prime Minister of Turkey for twelve years. So Erdogan's role in world politics would best be identified as a *chief prince*. Ezekiel 39:1 identifies the Antichrist as the "chief prince" or primary governor among the provinces of Turkey!

More from High Time to Awake

Available from Amazon.com, CreateSpace.com, and other retail outlets. Also available on Kindle and other devices.

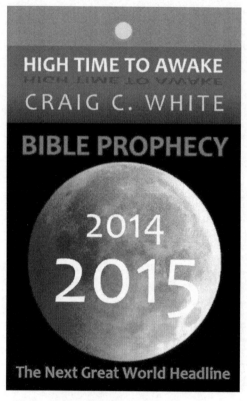

Bible Prophecy 2014-2015: Welcome to 2014. Bible prophecy is unfolding everywhere. The heathen are raging in the Middle East. Egyptian is fighting Egyptian. Christians are being killed and tormented more than ever. The New World Order is old news. An international security agreement and Palestinian state are being forged for the nation of Israel. All of these events have been foretold in bible prophecy. **Bible Prophecy 2014-2015** tells us what to expect in the coming two years.

www.hightimetoawake.com

Chapter Two

Alexis Tsipras is NOT the Antichrist!

Photo credit: Joanna - PIAZZA del POPOLO
www.flickr.com

By Craig C. White

Whoa! There seems to be a movement afoot that declares that Alexis Tsipras the new Prime Minister of Greece is a candidate for being the Antichrist. This observation is made without quoting one scripture reference. There is a popular idea that the Antichrist will win hearts and minds worldwide with his sparkling personality. It seems that people are jumping to conclusions about him because Prime Minister Tsipras is young and some say charismatic. The bible does not identify the Antichrist as either young or charismatic.

Alexis Tsipras is the new Prime Minister of Greece and the leader of the *Coalition of the Radical Left* called *SYRIZA*. Tsipras was first elected to the Greek Parliament in 2009. Greece has been driven into economic collapse by corrupt socialist government. Tsipras believes that Greece must now embrace absolute socialism. His initial efforts to seek debt forgiveness from the European Union have been rejected.

No I don't think that Alexis Tsipras is the Antichrist. But I am certain that he is an antichrist. He is an atheist. He thinks that Russia should conquer Ukraine. I think that he will promote the formation of a new European, Russian, and Middle Eastern (or Islamic) Union. Daniel chapter 7 tells us about this. Please read my commentary titled "The Leopard is Upon Us!" in my book "The Fall of Satan and Rise of the Antichrist".

So at first folks claimed that Alexis Tsipras may be the Antichrist. Now people are saying that Alexis Tsipras must have some small part of Jewish lineage. They say that the Antichrist must be Jewish in order to be received as a Jewish Messiah. Not only do I not agree that the Antichrist must be Jewish but I can't find any information that says that Alexis Tsipras is Jewish at all. Everything that I read about Alexis Tsipras says that he is Greek. If folks argued that Alexis Tsipras was the Antichrist because he was a gentile they would make a better case.

The Antichrist will be the ruler over the next world empire. Like most rulers of world empires throughout history he will be a tyrant. The Antichrist will not be warmly received as a Christian or a Jewish messiah. The title *Antichrist* doesn't mean that he will be a false Messiah rather the title *Antichrist* means "against" Christ. The Antichrist will show himself that he is god. He will also speak against the God of Israel. The Antichrist will perhaps be warmly received as a Muslim Mahdi.

2Thessalonians 2:4 Who opposeth and exalteth himself above all that is called God, or that is worshipped; so that he as God sitteth in the temple of God, shewing himself that he is God.

One world leader today has already proclaimed that he is god. That world leader is Turkish President Recep Tayyip Erdogan.

The Antichrist is like the ancient Assyrian kings. He will invade Syria and then he will invade northern Israel. Latter he will return to invade southern Israel (Isaiah 10). Turkish President Erdogan has vowed to overthrow the Assad government in Damascus, Syria.

The Antichrist is like Antiochus Epiphanes. He will invade Egypt and then Jerusalem during the Tribulation (Dan 11). Turkish President Erdogan wants to reinstall Muslim Brotherhood leadership in Egypt.

The Antichrist is the *chief prince* or Prime Minister or Turkey (Ezekiel 39). Erdogan was the Prime Minister of Turkey from 2002-2014.

The Antichrist will confirm a seven year treaty with many parties concerning Israel (Dan 9:27). The Turkey-Israeli reconciliation agreement remains unsigned.

There is one person on the world scene today that is very likely to fulfill all of these end times prophecies. He is Turkish President Recep Tayyip Erdogan.

Chapter Three

Saudi Prince Alwaleed bin Talal is NOT the Antichrist

Photo credit: Tribes of the World www.flickr.com

But Turkish President Erdogan is!

By Craig C. White

Saudi Arabia's Prince Alwaleed bin Talal is a wealthy business man. Lately he has been on a tour around Israel. The Prince is talking about a new level of cooperation between Saudi Arabia and Israel. Some folks are jumping to the conclusion that he may be the Antichrist.

Iran is Saudi Arabia's worst enemy. Iran is also Israel's enemy. Israel has the will and the ability to bomb Iran's nuclear processing facilities. That is why Saudi Arabia is being nice to Israel now.

In November 2014 Turkish Prime Minister Erdogan announced his plan to create a new Islamic Union. The first four nations that will most likely belong to this Islamic Union are Turkey, Syria, Iraq, and Iran. This Union is almost certainly the leopard described in Daniel 7:6. This Islamic Union will join together with the European Union as well as with the new Russian Union to form the next World Empire. The ruler of the next World Empire is the Antichrist. So in order for a Saudi Arabian Prince to become the ruler of the next World Empire he would need to participate in it. Turkish Prime Minister Erdogan specifically said that Saudi Arabia was the enemy of the new Islamic Union. It is doubtful that Saudi Arabia will even be allowed to be a part of the new Islamic Union or to participate in the next World Empire.

Saudi Prince Alwaleed bin Talal is not the Antichrist. He doesn't fulfill bible prophecy. But I know somebody who does! So let's identify the Antichrist by the bible prophecy that he fulfills.

According to Isaiah chapter 10 the Antichrist will invade Syria and then he will invade Israel just like the ancient Assyrian kings did. Turkish President Erdogan is the Antichrist. Right now he is sending troops and tanks towards Aleppo, Hamah, and Damascus in order to destroy Syria's capital city and to remove Syrian President Assad from power. Jeremiah 49:23 describes an invasion gathering against these Syrian cities. Jeremiah also predicts the ruin of Damascus.

Chapter Four

Erdogan is the Antichrist!

Photo credit: World Economic Forum

Antichrist overview

By Craig C. White

Since late last year Turkish Prime Minister Erdogan has been claiming that he is God and so have his supporters! According to the bible this is something that the Antichrist will do.

2Th 2:4 Who opposeth and exalteth himself above all that is called God, or that is worshipped; so that he as God sitteth in the temple of God, shewing himself that he is God.

Turkish Prime Minister Erdogan has also announced his plans to form of a new Islamic Union led by Turkey. Erdogan has made his desire to reestablish the Turkish ruled Ottoman Empire very clear. Erdogan has also vowed that he will remove Syrian President Bashar Assad from power. According to the bible the Antichrist will also do all of these things

The Antichrist will do many other things. So will Prime Minister Erdogan. Turkish Prime Minister Erdogan is the Antichrist. Here is why, and here is why the Antichrist will destroy Damascus and then invade Israel!

First the Antichrist is called the Assyrian in Isaiah chapter 10 and elsewhere. The Antichrist isn't called *the Assyrian* because he will be from Assyria or northern Iraq. The Antichrist is called the Assyrian because he will do the same things that the Assyrian kings did! The Assyrian Kings led two separate invasions into Israel. First they invaded Syria plus northern Israel in 734 BC. Second they invaded southern Israel in 701 BC.

You would probably say that Isaiah chapter 17 is about the future destruction of Damascus, and you would be right. But Isaiah chapter 17 is foremost about the conquest of the country of Syria in 734 BC by you know who: The Assyrian King Tiglath-pileser! This is a model for the future destruction of Damascus.

For verse by verse commentary through Isaiah chapter 17 please read my commentary titled "Isaiah 17 predicts the destruction of Damascus" in my book "Nation by Nation Verse by Verse".

The verses below describe the second Assyrian invasion into Israel. They also describe the future invasion of Israel by the Antichrist. Guess what? He is bragging about his previous conquest of Syria and of northern Israel!

Isaiah 10:7-11 Howbeit he meaneth not so, neither doth his heart think so; but it is in his heart to destroy and cut off nations not a few. 8 For he saith, Are not my princes altogether kings? 9 Is not Calno as Carchemish? is not Hamath as Arpad? is not Samaria as Damascus? 10 As my hand hath found the kingdoms of the idols, and whose graven images did excel them of Jerusalem and of Samaria; 11 Shall I not, as I have done unto Samaria and her idols, so do to Jerusalem and her idols?

Assyrian King Sennacherib is speaking in the previous verses. So is the future invader of Israel. He is recalling previous victories over Syria and over northern Israel.

It is looking more and more like Turkey will invade Syria soon. That's because newly elected Turkish President Erdogan is the Antichrist!

For more please read my commentary "The Assyrian is the Antichrist!" in my book "Turkey invades Israel – Halfway to Armageddon".

Here is the second reason why Erdogan is the Antichrist. In Ezekiel chapter 39 the Antichrist invades Israel. This is the battle of Armageddon. Ezekiel calls the future invader of Israel *Magog*. Magog is the Antichrist and Erdogan is Magog! Ezekiel 38:2-3 calls Magog the "chief prince" amongst his brothers. The Hebrew words that are translated as "chief prince" mean "primary governor". Magog's brothers settled Turkey and were set over provinces. Most bible prophecy teachers place them there. Magog was also set over a province in Turkey. He was the most prominent prince amongst his brothers. So the end time invader of Israel called *Magog* is the "primary governor" of Turkey. I feel comfortable calling him the Prime Minister of Turkey don't you?

Eze 38:1-3 And the word of the LORD came unto me, saying, 2 Son of man, set thy face against Gog, the land of Magog, the chief prince of Meshech and Tubal, and prophesy against him, 3 And say, Thus saith the Lord GOD; Behold, I *am* against thee, O Gog, the chief prince of Meshech and Tubal:

To learn more about the identity of Magog and his brothers please read my commentary titled "Princes of Turkey" in my book "Turkey invades Israel – Halfway to Armageddon".

According to Ezekiel chapters 38 & 39 Magog leads two separate end time invasions into Israel. Ezekiel chapter 38 describes a Turkish led battle joined by Iran, Libya, and Sudan. Ezekiel chapter 39 obviously describes the battle of Armageddon. So if Magog leads the battle described in Ezekiel chapter 39, and the Antichrist leads the battle of Armageddon then Magog is the Antichrist. Let's not forget that these two invasions are modeled after the past Assyrian invasions. The first Assyrian invasion started with an invasion into Syria followed by an invasion into northern Israel. The second Assyrian invasion went into southern Israel. What's the point of knowing that the Antichrist is called *the Assyrian* if we are just going to ignore it? The Antichrist will invade Syria plus northern Israel. He will then come back later to invade southern Israel. These are the battles of Gog and Magog described in Ezekiel chapters 38 and 39.

For more about the people and places involved in the battle of Gog and Magog please read my commentary titled "Magog Made Easier!" in my book "Turkey invades Israel – Halfway to Armageddon".

The Antichrist is also called a "prince" and "a little horn". Magog is called the "chief prince". If a big horn is a king, then a little horn is a prince! A Prime Minister is a "chief prince"! New elected Turkish President Erdogan was the Prime Minister of Turkey from 2002 to December 2014!

Third Libya, Iran, and Sudan are all fighting in Syria today! This is a list of the nations that the Prime Minister of Turkey will lead in an invasion into Israel according to Ezekiel 38:5!

Ezekiel 38:5 Persia, Ethiopia, and Libya with them; all of them with shield and helmet:

So Erdogan will invade Syria, destroy Damascus, and then lead these armies in an Invasion into Israel. It will not go well for them. Some sort of seven year Turkey-Israeli peace plan will be put in place. Erdogan will break this treaty in the middle of its term. Then it's welcome to the Great Tribulation! Somewhere along this timeline Jesus Christ will come back for his Church. I am going with him.

For more please read my commentary titled "Who is fighting in Syria?" in my book "Turkey invades Israel – Halfway to Armageddon".

Fourth Turkish President Erdogan is honoring the military might of the Turkish led Ottoman Empire in his new palace (see Daniel 11:37-38 below). The Erdogan palace is the largest palace in the world. Erdogan has dedicated his palace to the resurgence of Turkey as a world power. He proudly displays Turkish soldiers dressed up in Ottoman era armor. By the way President Erdogan has publicly announced his intention to reestablish a Turkish led Islamic Empire!

Daniel 11:37-38 Neither shall he regard the God of his fathers, nor the desire of women, nor regard any god: for he shall magnify himself above all. 38 But in his estate shall he honour the God of forces: and a god whom his fathers knew not shall he honour with gold,

and silver, and with precious stones, and pleasant things.

Please read my commentary titled "Erdogan is honoring the God of forces in the Erdogan Palace" in my book "Welcome to the end times".

Erdogan is the Antichrist. He will be the ruler of the next World Empire. Jesus Christ will destroy it at his second coming. Before that Jesus Christ is coming to take his Church away to heaven. That means that Jesus is coming back very very soon!

Rev 22:20-21 He which testifieth these things saith, Surely I come quickly. Amen. Even so, come, Lord Jesus. 21 The grace of our Lord Jesus Christ be with you all. Amen.

God bless you, Craig C. White

Chapter Five

Antichrist checklist

Check out Turkish President Erdogan

By Craig C. White

The world has gone haywire! Folks are beginning to conclude that we are all entering the end times spoken of in the bible. They are right! The end times are marked by terrible wars and natural disasters, by the oppression of Israel, and by the rise of a World Empire. The ruler of this World Empire is known as the Antichrist. Now more than ever folks are expecting to identify the Antichrist. They have several candidates but only one world leader is fulfilling the criteria that the bible lays out.

Turkish President Recep Tayyip Erdogan is the Antichrist. Here is a checklist that shows which bible prophecies he has already fulfilled.

✓ The Antichrist will claim that he is god.

2Th 2:4 Who opposeth and exalteth himself above all that is called God, or that is worshipped; so that he as God sitteth in the temple of God, shewing himself that he is God.

Lately Turkish President Erdogan has been claiming to be god! There is even a public campaign in Turkey claiming that Erdogan is god. Erdogan's AKP Party rewrote the Turkish national anthem adding the line, "Erdogan always gets his power from Allah". Billboards in Istanbul invite the people to attend Erdogan's "holy" birthday celebration. Turkish President Erdogan along with his supporters is continuing to claim that Erdogan is a deity.

Antichrist checklist copyright 2015 Craig C. White

hightimetoawake.com

HIGH TIME TO AWAKE

BIBLE PROPHECY with CRAIG C. WHITE

Antichrist checklist
By Craig C. White

Turkish President Recep Tayyip Erdogan is the Antichrist. Here is a checklist that shows which bible prophecies he has already fulfilled.

- ✓ The Antichrist will claim that he is god (2Th 2:4).

- ✓ The Antichrist will perform false miracles (2Th 2:9)

- ✓ The Antichrist will invade Syria and then northern Israel (Isaiah 10:5-6).

- ✓ The end time invader of Israel is the primary governor of Turkey (Eze 38:1-3).

- ✓ The Antichrist is also called a "prince" and "a little horn" (Dan 7:8).

- ✓ The Antichrist will build his palace between the seas on top of a holy mountain (Dan 11:45).

- ✓ The Antichrist will honor the god of military power in his palace (Daniel 11:37-38).

It's High Time to Awake!

✓ The Antichrist will perform false miracles.

2Th 2:9 Even him, whose coming is after the working of Satan with all power and signs and lying wonders,

Guess what? Turkish President Erdogan is now performing public healings. During an outdoor pre-election rally in May 2015 President Erdogan addressed tens of thousands of his party supporters. During his speech a woman fainted in the front row. The woman was carried to Erdogan where he touched her. The woman instantly revived and began praising Allah. Erdogan is performing false miracles.

✓ The Antichrist will invade Syria and then northern Israel.

Isaiah 10:5-6 O Assyrian, the rod of mine anger, and the staff in their hand is mine indignation. 6 I will send him against an hypocritical nation, and against the people of my wrath will I give him a charge, to take the spoil, and to take the prey, and to tread them down like the mire of the streets.

The Antichrist is called "the Assyrian" in Isaiah because he will do the same things that the Assyrian kings did! The Assyrian Kings led two separate invasions into Israel. First they invaded Syria plus northern Israel in 734 BC. The second Assyrian invasion was into southern Israel in 701 BC.

Turkish President Erdogan vowed that he will remove Syrian President Bashar Assad from power in Damascus. He also called for Islam to conquer Jerusalem.

I expect Turkish President Erdogan to invade Syria, wipe out Damascus, and to then lead the forces that are now fighting in Syria into northern Israel.

✓ The end time invader of Israel is the primary governor of Turkey.

Eze 38:1-3 And the word of the LORD came unto me, saying, 2 Son of man, set thy face against Gog, the land of Magog, the chief prince of Meshech and Tubal, and prophesy against him, 3 And say, Thus saith the Lord GOD; Behold, I am against thee, O Gog, the chief prince of Meshech and Tubal.

According to Ezekiel chapter 38 a man called "Magog" will lead an invasion into Israel. Ezekiel calls this end time invader of Israel the "chief prince" amongst his brothers. The Hebrew words translated as "chief prince" mean "primary governor". Magog and his brothers settled Turkey and were set over provinces. Most bible prophecy teachers place them there. Magog was also set over a province in Turkey. He was the most prominent prince amongst his brothers. So the end time invader of Israel is the "primary governor" of Turkey. I feel comfortable in calling him the Prime Minister of Turkey don't you!? Recep Tayyip Erdogan was the Prime Minister of Turkey from 2012 until December 2014.

✔ The Antichrist is also called a "prince" and "a little horn".

Dan 7:8 I considered the horns, and, behold, there came up among them another little horn, before whom there were three of the first horns plucked up by the roots: and, behold, in this horn were eyes like the eyes of man, and a mouth speaking great things.

Magog is called the "chief prince" of Turkey in Ezekiel. He is also called a "little horn". If a big horn is a king, then a little horn is a prince! A Prime Minister is a "chief prince"! Now President Erdogan was Prime Minister of Turkey for 12 years.

✔ The Antichrist will build his palace between the seas on top of a holy mountain.

Dan 11:45 And he shall plant the tabernacles of his palace between the seas in the glorious holy mountain; yet he shall come to his end, and none shall help him

Erdogan has built the largest palace in the world for himself in Turkey's capital city of Ankara. It is called the "White Palace". It sits on top of the highest hill overlooking Ankara. The White Palace is built in a preserved area of land that was dedicated to Suleyman Shah the grandfather of the founder of the Ottoman Empire. It is illegal to build on the preserve but Erdogan built there anyway. Erdogan's presidential palace is built between the Mediterranean Sea, the Black Sea, and the Caspian Sea.

✓ The Antichrist will honor the god of military power in his palace.

Daniel 11:37-38 Neither shall he regard the God of his fathers, nor the desire of women, nor regard any god: for he shall magnify himself above all. 38 But in his estate shall he honour the God of forces: and a god whom his fathers knew not shall he honour with gold, and silver, and with precious stones, and pleasant things.

Turkish President Erdogan is honoring the military might of the Turkish led Ottoman Empire in his new palace. Erdogan has dedicated his palace to the resurgence of Turkey as a world power. Around his palace Erdogan proudly displays Turkish soldiers that are dressed in Ottoman era armor. By the way President Erdogan has publicly announced his intention to reestablish a Turkish led Ottoman Empire or Islamic Caliphate!

More from High Time to Awake

Available from Amazon.com, CreateSpace.com, and other retail outlets. Also available on Kindle and other devices.

Just before Israel's seven year period of Tribulation the nations of the old world will fight against one another.

Luke 21:10 Then said he unto them, Nation shall rise against nation, and kingdom against kingdom:

Nation by Nation Verse by Verse identifies a few key nations who will play significant roles during the years leading up to and during Israel's time of trouble. We will take a verse by verse look at specific prophetic events that these nations will fulfill. I expect that these prophecies reflect the near time future of world history.

www.hightimetoawake.com

Chapter Six

Leopard map update!

Turkey, Syria, Iraq, and Iran

Daniel 7:6

By Craig C. White

Hello bible prophecy watchers. Daniel chapter 7 describes the formation of four kingdoms each represented by a specific wild animal or *beast*. The first three kingdoms or Unions combine to form the forth kingdom or World Empire. In Daniel 7:6 a kingdom is formed that is represented by a leopard. I think that the leopard in Daniel chapter 7 is a Middle Eastern Union. I think that it will be formed shortly.

I updated my "Look for an Islamic Union represented by a leopard" map. I added black outlines around the four nations that I think will first form this Union. The lighter shaded nations are likely contenders to become secondary members. Also see the new map legend at the bottom of the map.

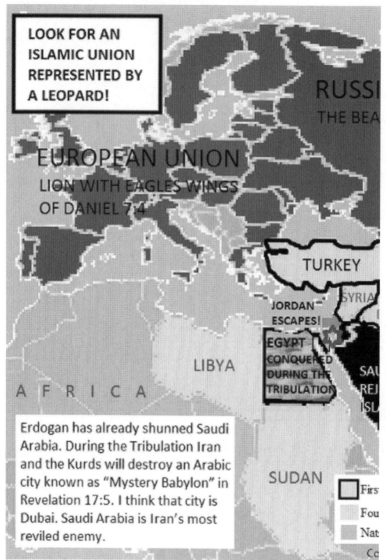

LOOK FOR AN ISLAMIC UNION REPRESENTED BY A LEOPARD!

EUROPEAN UNION
LION WITH EAGLES WINGS
OF DANIEL 7:4

RUSSI
THE BEA

TURKEY

SYRIA

JORDAN ESCAPES!

EGYPT CONQUERED DURING THE TRIBULATION

LIBYA

AFRICA

SAU
REJ
ISL

Erdogan has already shunned Saudi Arabia. During the Tribulation Iran and the Kurds will destroy an Arabic city known as "Mystery Babylon" in Revelation 17:5. I think that city is Dubai. Saudi Arabia is Iran's most reviled enemy.

SUDAN

Firs
Fou
Nat
Cc

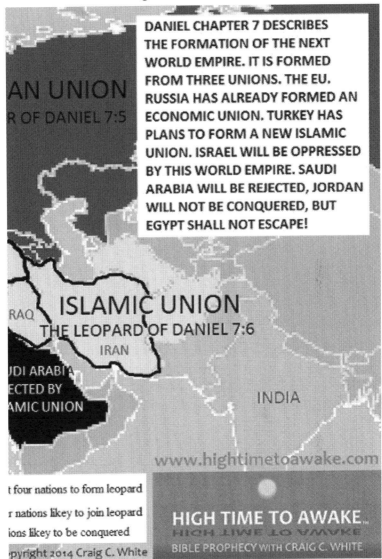

DANIEL CHAPTER 7 DESCRIBES THE FORMATION OF THE NEXT WORLD EMPIRE. IT IS FORMED FROM THREE UNIONS. THE EU. RUSSIA HAS ALREADY FORMED AN ECONOMIC UNION. TURKEY HAS PLANS TO FORM A NEW ISLAMIC UNION. ISRAEL WILL BE OPPRESSED BY THIS WORLD EMPIRE. SAUDI ARABIA WILL BE REJECTED, JORDAN WILL NOT BE CONQUERED, BUT EGYPT SHALL NOT ESCAPE!

AN UNION
R OF DANIEL 7:5

ISLAMIC UNION
THE LEOPARD OF DANIEL 7:6
IRAQ
IRAN

JDI ARABI
ECTED BY
MIC UNION

INDIA

www.hightimetoawake.com

t four nations to form leopard
r nations likey to join leopard
ions likey to be conquered
pyright 2014 Craig C. White

HIGH TIME TO AWAKE.
BIBLE PROPHECY WITH CRAIG C. WHITE

Copyright 2014 Craig C. White

I think that Turkey, Syria, Iraq, and Iran will be the first nations that form the new Middle East Union that will be represented by a leopard.

Dan 7:6 After this I beheld, and lo another, like a leopard, which had upon the back of it four wings of a

fowl; the beast had also four heads; and dominion was given to it.

I wrote my commentary titled "The Leopard is Upon Us!" way back in 2011. Since then the identity of the four primary nations of the leopard in Daniel 7:6 has become more apparent. In November 2014 then Turkish Prime Minister Erdogan announced his plans to form a new Islamic Union. I think that the first four nations to be included in this Union will be Turkey, Syria, Iraq, and Iran. These are the same four nations that Revelation 9:13-16 identifies as being located along the Euphrates River. During the first half of the seven year Tribulation period these four nations along with four other secondary nations (or perhaps four Terrorist organizations) will conquer most of the Middle East, Northern Africa, and Central Asia. Please read my commentary titled "World War III" in my book "Welcome to the end times".

Rev 9:13-16 And the sixth angel sounded, and I heard a voice from the four horns of the golden altar which is before God, 14 Saying to the sixth angel which had the trumpet, Loose the four angels which are bound in the great river Euphrates. 15 And the four angels were loosed, which were prepared for an hour, and a day, and a month, and a year, for to slay the third part of men. 16 And the number of the army of the horsemen were two hundred thousand thousand: and I heard the number of them.

Recently elected President Erdogan has made his intentions of forming a Turkish ruled revived Ottoman Empire with him as its Sultan very clear! The first nation to fall to Erdogan and to the Turkish Army will be Syria. After Damascus is destroyed and Syria is conquered then Erdogan will install Muslim Brotherhood leadership in Syria! Next the leopard (or Islamic Union) will be formed.

Chapter Seven

The little horn is a big pain

Fill in the blank:

If a *big horn* is a king, then a *little horn* is a _____.

Daniel 7:8

By Craig C. White

Who is the little horn in Daniel 7:8? Well we are given a clue to his identity in Daniel 8:9. The little horn in Daniel 7:8 isn't the same person as the little horn in Daniel 8:9, but they do have similarities. At the time it was written Daniel 8:9 was about events in the future. Those events were fulfilled during the time of the Grecian Empire. Looking back we can see who the little horn was and we can know a little about him. We know that a Grecian prince named Antiochus Epiphanies manipulated his way onto the throne of the Seleucid dynasty. The Seleucid dynasty was one fourth of the Grecian empire headquartered in Syria. Prince Antiochus Epiphanies became king. Antiochus Epiphanies was the little horn in Daniel 8:9. The little horn in Daniel 7:8 is also a prince who will become the king of the next World Empire. The final gentile ruled World Empire is also known as the New World Order. It will be in power during the 7 year Tribulation period. All or part of the Tribulation period happens after the Rapture of the Church.

Dan 7:8 I considered the horns, and, behold, there came up among them another little horn, before whom there were three of the first horns plucked up by the roots: and, behold, in this horn *were* eyes like the eyes of man, and a mouth speaking great things.

What is a little horn? Horns commonly represent kings in bible prophecy. A little horn is a secondary leader, for instance a prince, vice-president, or governor. This little horn will evidently take away or usurp the authority of three out of ten kings that have been set over the next

World Empire. The *little horn* will then become the ultimate authority of the next World Empire. This little horn has a *mouth speaking great things*. He blasphemes God, *showing himself that he is God* (Daniel 11:36-37). This little horn is obviously the Antichrist (1 John 2:18). By the way, the Antichrist will do many of the same things that Antiochus Epiphanies did.

Chapter Eight

Does the Antichrist know that he is the son of perdition?

By Craig C. White

This commentary was written to answer a "High Time to Awake" reader's questions. The reader asks, what is preventing the revealing the Antichrist? Does he know that this is his destiny? Will he be able to say no? And finally, why do so many believe that the Antichrist is Satan incarnate?

2Th 2:3 Let no man deceive you by any means: for *that day shall not come,* except there come a falling away first, and that man of sin be revealed, the son of perdition;

In the verse above, the Antichrist is called the *son of perdition*. The word *perdition* means *destruction*. The word translated as *son* is the Greek word uihos (hwee-os') meaning *heir*. So the Antichrist is the inheritor of destruction. Does he know this? Like every unbeliever who shares in his fate the Antichrist does not believe God. So I doubt that he believes that he is doomed for destruction. *Apoleia* is the Greek word translated as *perdition*. Here is the definition of *Apoleia* from the Strong Greek Dictionary.

apoleia, ap-o'-li-a
ruin or loss (physical, spiritual or eternal): – damnable (-nation), destruction, die, perdition, X perish, pernicious ways, waste.

One of Jesus' disciples was also called the *son of perdition*. Judas Iscariot gave Jesus to the Romans to be killed. His inheritance was death and hell.

Joh 17:12 While I was with them in the world, I kept them in thy name: those that thou gavest me I have

kept, and none of them is lost, but the son of perdition; that the scripture might be fulfilled.

Joh 6:70-71 Jesus answered them, Have not I chosen you twelve, and one of you is a devil? 71 He spake of Judas Iscariot the son of Simon: for he it was that should betray him, being one of the twelve.

Satan on the other hand has a notion that his time is short and that his fate is sure.

Rev 12:12 Therefore rejoice, *ye* heavens, and ye that dwell in them. Woe to the inhabiters of the earth and of the sea! for the devil is come down unto you, having great wrath, because he knoweth that he hath but a short time.

What is preventing the revealing of the Antichrist? The Antichrist is only a man who is empowered by Satan. Satan has had access to God's heavenly thrown for a long time. He accuses believers in the God of Israel of being unfaithful (Rev 12:10). At some point soon Satan will be cast out of heaven for good.

Rev 12:8-9 And prevailed not; neither was their place found any more in heaven. 9 And the great dragon was cast out, that old serpent, called the Devil, and Satan, which deceiveth the whole world: he was cast out into the earth, and his angels were cast out with him.

Look back up at 2Th 2:3. The phrase "a falling away" refers to Satan's fall from heaven to earth. After Satan is cast out of heaven by God he will be available to empower the man called the *son of perdition*. His main goal will be the subjection of the world to himself and also the destruction of the nation of Israel. So the fall of Satan precedes the revealing of the Antichrist on earth. The revealing of the Antichrist also precedes the Tribulation period and may precede the Rapture of the Church!

2Th 2:8-9 And then shall that Wicked be revealed, whom the Lord shall consume with the spirit of his mouth, and shall destroy with the brightness of his coming: 9 *Even him,* whose coming is after the working of Satan with all power and signs and lying wonders,

After Satan falls and then empowers this man then the Antichrist will be revealed on earth. The revealing of the Antichrist will occur by way of false miracles, blasphemy against the God of Israel or by his sitting in the temple of God *showing himself that he is god.*

2Th 2:3-4 Let no man deceive you by any means: for *that day shall not come,* except there come a falling away first, and that man of sin be revealed, the son of perdition; 4 Who opposeth and exalteth himself above all that is called God, or that is worshipped; so that he as God sitteth in the temple of God, shewing himself that he is God.

In Isaiah chapter 10 the future Antichrist is compared to the ancient Assyrian kings. Isaiah describes the invasion of Israel. I think that like the Assyrian kings the Antichrist will invade Syria and destroy Damascus. He will then lead an invasion into Israel. I think that we are about to see this happen. The following verses describe the Assyrian kings as well as the future Antichrist. Look at verse 7. This person doesn't realize that he will destroy Israel and also destroy many other nations as well.

Isa 10:5-7 O Assyrian, the rod of mine anger, and the staff in their hand is mine indignation. 6 I will send him against an hypocritical nation, and against the people of my wrath will I give him a charge, to take the spoil, and to take the prey, and to tread them down like the mire of the streets. 7 Howbeit he meaneth not so, neither doth his heart think so; but *it is* in his heart to destroy and cut off nations not a few.

In Isaiah below, Satan is pictured in his judgment. He has been cast into hell. I think that this may refer to his 1000 year exile into hell after the second coming of Jesus Christ. Isaiah may also refer to the man known as the Antichrist in his judgment. I think that verse 16 is saying that the other occupants of hell will down look on him and think, "Did this mere man cause so much destruction?" In verses 18-20 the man called the Antichrist will become king of a World Empire but he will not receive the dignity of burial at a grave site.

Isa 14:15-20 Yet thou shalt be brought down to hell, to the sides of the pit. 16 They that see thee shall narrowly look upon thee, *and* consider thee, *saying, Is* this the man that made the earth to tremble, that did shake kingdoms; 17 *That* made the world as a wilderness, and destroyed the cities thereof; *that* opened not the house of his prisoners? 18 All the kings of the nations, *even* all of them, lie in glory, every one in his own house. 19 But thou art cast out of thy grave like an abominable branch, *and as* the raiment of those that are slain, thrust through with a sword, that go down to the stones of the pit; as a carcase trodden under feet. 20 Thou shalt not be joined with them in burial, because thou hast destroyed thy land, *and* slain thy people: the seed of evildoers shall never be renowned.

The *son of perdition* will seek his own personal glory but he will inherit destruction. At Christ's second coming Jesus will toss the Antichrist into a lake of fire while he is ALIVE, body and soul.

Rev 19:20 And the beast was taken, and with him the false prophet that wrought miracles before him, with which he deceived them that had received the mark of the beast, and them that worshipped his image. These both were cast alive into a lake of fire burning with brimstone.

The Antichrist is only a man who is empowered by Satan after Satan is cast out of heaven forever.

Chapter Nine

Revelation 13 – Image of the beast

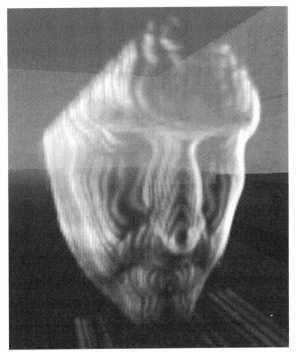

Image credit: Ian Truelove www.flickr.com/

The case of the haunted hologram!

Revelation 13

By Craig C. White

This is a commentary on Revelation 13. I am explaining the entire chapter mostly just to tell you about the image of the beast described in Revelation 13:15. In this case the beast isn't a scary animal; instead it is the next World Empire. The image of the beast is literally some sort of picture or statue that represents the next World Empire or perhaps looks like its leader. The world may have already had its first glimpse of this beast's image. You may not agree with everything that I have to say; nevertheless I think you will find this enlightening. Allow me to state that I am not

47

certain that I have all of the facts yet, but I do have a lot of them. OK now let's all make certain that our socks are pulled on tightly!

The Apostle John is writing this around 94 AD. He is having a vision about conditions on earth during the time of the seven year Tribulation period. It is a time of trouble for Israel and a time of God's judgment against the nations of the world. A final man-ruled World Empire has formed on the earth. John sees a beast rise up out of the sea. The beast represents all of the World Empires throughout history. The sea represents the nations of the world.

Revelation 13:1a And I stood upon the sand of the sea, and saw a beast rise up out of the sea,

In bible prophecy a beast represents a gentile body of government. Gentile simply means the *nations*. A gentile government is ruled by men and not by God. A beast could represent a nation, or union of nations, or in this case a world empire. As we will see latter a beast can also represent the governmental body of a world religion. A beast is a large governmental body. When that government is ruled by one man; a beast can also refer to that one certain man.

The Apostle John sees a beast with seven heads. Many bible scholars agree that these seven heads represent the seven World Empires that have formed on earth throughout world history. These world empires are in order; the Egyptian, Assyrian, Babylonian, Mede-Persian, Grecian, Roman, and the Ottoman Turkish Empire. Now there is a lot of debate about the last one. Most scholars say that the last head represents the final World Empire yet to come. Almost everybody says that the final head represents a revived Roman Empire in the future. I have said that myself, but always with reservation. I think that the seventh head more likely represents the Ottoman Turkish Empire. It could in fact also represent a revived Ottoman Turkish Empire of the future. Suffice it to say that the seventh head most certainly represents an end time (Tribulation period) World Empire.

Revelation 13:1b having seven heads and ten horns, and upon his horns ten crowns, and upon his heads the name of blasphemy.

Horns commonly represent kings in bible prophecy. The ten horns are ten kings that rule over the final World Empire. This is explained in Daniel 7:24 and Revelation 17:12. Every World Empire or kingdom has been ruled by men in rebellion to God. Before any of these World Empires existed, God scattered men from forming a man ruled World Government at the tower of Babel (Gen 11:1-9). Ever since God confused the language at the tower of Babel men have sought to undo God's work there. Satan has always been the driving force behind the formation of World Empires. He wants to be worshiped like the most High God (Isa 14:14); and to become king over the nations of the earth.

Revelation 13:2 And the beast which I saw was like unto a leopard, and his feet were as the feet of a bear, and his mouth as the mouth of a lion: and the dragon gave him his power, and his seat, and great authority.

In the verse above, the apostle John sees a beast whose body parts are like a leopard and a bear and a lion. Daniel chapter 7 describes the formation of this multi animal beast (or World Empire). For now let me tell you that this strange beast is the in fact the final man-ruled World Empire that rules over the earth during the Tribulation period. It is the same World Empire that is represented by the seventh head in Revelation 13:1. This final World Empire is made of three smaller groups of nations or Unions. I think that the leopard represents a Middle Eastern Union, the bear represents a Russian Union, and the lion represents England along with the European Union. These three Unions will unite to form the next World Empire. Please read my outstanding commentary on Daniel chapter 7 titled

"The Leopard is Upon Us!" in my book "The Fall of Satan and Rise of the Antichrist". Now I want to continue so I can tell you about the strange image of the beast described in Revelation 13:15.

Revelation 13:3 And I saw one of his heads as it were wounded to death; and his deadly wound was healed: and all the world wondered after the beast.

There is a lot of debate concerning Revelation 13:3 above. Many folks say that the king of the final World Empire will receive a bloody wound (or booboo) in his head. But I don't think so. Please allow me to remind you that in this example the heads of the beast represent World Empires and not kings. Kings are represented by horns. The empire is wounded not the king. I think that John is describing a revived World Empire. This could be a revived Ottoman Turkish Empire or maybe a revived Roman Empire. In the verse above, the nations of the world are impressed with the next World Empire.

In the verse below, the word translated as *worship* is a little misleading. The word worship used here describes an outward demonstration of homage. It literally describes a dog licking his master's hand. So the world won't necessarily reverence the next World Empire, but the world will show subservience to it. I can imagine that a World Empire including Europe, the Middle East, and Russia would be seen as the greatest power amongst the world's nations.

Revelation 13:4 And they worshipped the dragon which gave power unto the beast: and they worshipped the beast, saying, Who is like unto the beast? who is able to make war with him?

It hasn't been explained here but the next World Empire will ultimately be ruled by one man (Daniel 7:8). By the way, I think that that man is Turkish President Erdogan. Satan is behind this World Empire. He will give its ruler the ability to say bad things about the God of Israel. Perhaps this ruler will give persuasive speeches. He will rule the next World Empire for 42 months. During this three and a half year period he will oppress the nation of Israel (Dan 7:25). This is known as the Great Tribulation period (Mat 24:21).

Revelation 13:5 And there was given unto him a mouth speaking great things and blasphemies; and power was given unto him to continue forty and two months.

The ruler of the next World Empire will speak against God, and against his dwelling place, and against everybody who lives with him in heaven. This may be a reference to Church age believers who have just been resurrected and taken up into heaven at the Rapture. The whole world will be well aware of this event. Now most world leaders aren't compelled to insult people in heaven. But then the folks in heaven will be an undeniable sign that the God of Israel and his son Jesus Christ is about to judge the unbelieving world.

Revelation 13:6 And he opened his mouth in blasphemy against God, to blaspheme his name, and his tabernacle, and them that dwell in heaven.

In verse 7 below the term *the saints* refer to the nation of Israel. "To overcome them" means that he will kill the people of Israel. The ruler of the next World Empire will subdue and destroy much of the nation of Israel.

Revelation 13:7 And it was given unto him to make war with the saints, and to overcome them: and power was given him over all kindreds, and tongues, and nations.

The ruler of the next World Empire will have influence and authority over the people groups of the world. This doesn't necessarily mean that he will rule the entire world. The "nations" in verse 7 above refers to the original families that settled the old world after Noah's flood. These are the nations that are located around Israel. The next World Empire will cover the same geographic area that every ancient World Empire covered. That is between Europe and India.

Revelation 13:8 And all that dwell upon the earth shall worship him, whose names are not written in the book of life of the Lamb slain from the foundation of the world.

Read verse 8 carefully. It doesn't say that every person on earth will worship the ruler of the next World Empire. Instead it says that every non-Christian will worship the ruler of the next World Empire. The word translated as worship is the same word used in verse 4. It describes an outward demonstration of homage.

Revelation 13:9 If any man have an ear, let him hear. 10 He that leadeth into captivity shall go into captivity: he that killeth with the sword must be killed with the sword. Here is the patience and the faith of the saints.

Let me explain the verse above. This is a warning to every person and nation that either takes the people of Israel captive or kills any Jewish person during the Great Tribulation period. Jesus Christ will return and treat Israel's enemies in the same way that they have treated the people of Israel. He will kill them and send them to hell. Israel will survive as they remember God's faithfulness towards them. Please read my commentary titled "Jerusalem's Great Tribulation" in my book "Bible Prophecy 2014-2015".

Revelation 13:11 And I beheld another beast coming up out of the earth; and he had two horns like a lamb, and he spake as a dragon.

Hey I see different animal! By now you should know what a beast represents. A beast represents a large governmental body. It could be a nation, or union of nations, or an empire. It could also be a World Religion. I think that in this case a beast represents a World Religion. You should also know that horns represent kings. So this World Religion has two rulers. Jesus Christ is called the Lamb in Revelation 13:8. In Revelation 13:11 the lamb indicates that this World Religion looks like the Christian Church. The dragon indicates that it is empowered by Satan and that it preaches against God. The dragon also represents the seven headed beast referenced in Revelation 13:1. This dragon represents every World Empire throughout history. The beast of Revelation 13:11 is a World Religion that causes people to worship the next World Empire. Satan is the power behind every World Empire. He wants to subjugate men and to be worshiped as king of this world.

So a false World Religion will arise alongside of the next World Empire. This has been the case during every ancient World Empire. This false religion is less about worshiping God and more about denying God and also about bringing people under subjection to the World Empire.

Revelation 13:12 And he exerciseth all the power of the first beast before him, and causeth the earth and them which dwell therein to worship the first beast, whose deadly wound was healed.

We are still talking about the new wild animal or false World Religion. Remember that the World Religion has two leaders (or horns). This false religion also has been given authority to it by the next World Empire. The false religion will cause people to show outward submission to the World Empire. The bible often uses the terminology of "those who dwell on the earth" to refer to unbelievers or unbelieving nations. Revelation 13:12 probably refers to the non-Christian nations around Israel.

Revelation 13:13 And he doeth great wonders, so that he maketh fire come down from heaven on the earth in the sight of men,

It seems that the two leaders of the false religion will produce miraculous signs to prove their authority. They will make fire come from the sky to the ground in front of witnesses. I think that this refers to some sort of ceremonial action. The two leaders of the false religion will produce this sign during a religious service.

Most folks see the False Prophet represented in this verse. That seems likely to me. He may be the main culprit here but I would like to remind you that the false religion has two leaders (Revelation 13:11).

Revelation 19:20 And the beast was taken, and with him the false prophet that wrought miracles before him, with which he deceived them that had received the mark of the beast, and them that worshipped his image. These both were cast alive into a lake of fire burning with brimstone.

I am going out on a limb here but I suspect one person who is now on the world scene as being the prime candidate for fulfilling the role of the False Prophet. He is a prominent Muslim cleric named Fethullah Gulen. He wants to rule the world and is challenging Turkish President Erdogan for control over Turkey.

In the verse below, the false religion (or False Prophet) causes the non-Christian nations around Israel to stray from the truth of the God of Israel. He instructs them to make a likeness of the revived World Empire or perhaps more specifically of its ruler. An image is simply a representation of something, like a picture or statue. In this case it is some sort of idol to be worshiped. Its purpose is for the worship of the World Empire, or of its ruler as God. Here is the definition of the Greek word translated as image in Revelation 13:14 from the Strong Hebrew-Greek dictionary.

Image, eikōn, i-kone'

a likeness, that is, (literally) statue, profile, or (figuratively) representation, resemblance: – image.

Revelation 13:14 And deceiveth them that dwell on the earth by the means of those miracles which he had power to do in the sight of the beast; saying to them that dwell on the earth, that they should make an image to the beast, which had the wound by a sword, and did live.

I am going to assume that this image is in the likeness of the ruler of the next World Empire. That would mean that this image is probably a picture or statue of a man. In verse 15 below, we are told that this image can speak. So perhaps it would be more accurate to assume that this image is a moving picture or perhaps even something like a moving hologram with broadcasted sound! It seems to me that that would fulfill the parameters of a speaking representation of a man. If only something like that existed today. Guess what it does. Not only does a speaking hologram of a man exist, but a ten foot tall holographic image of Turkish Prime Minister Erdogan was employed recently to give an awe-inspiring speech to a stadium full of his supporters. In case you don't already know, Turkish Prime Minister Erdogan has ambitions to be the new Sultan of a revived Turkish Ottoman Empire. I think that Ezekiel chapters 38 and 39 indicate that a Turkish Prime Minister will lead two multinational invasions into Israel during the end time. Ezekiel chapter 39 describes the same invasion known as the battle of Armageddon. So I think that Turkish Prime Minister Erdogan is the prime suspect to become the ruler of the next World Empire. Please read my commentaries titled "Magog Made Easy!" and "Magog Made Easier!" in my book "Turkey invades Israel – Halfway to Armageddon".

Revelation 13:15 And he had power to give life unto the image of the beast, that the image of the beast should

both speak, and cause that as many as would not worship the image of the beast should be killed.

We are still talking about the false World Religion or the False Prophet and their work with the image of the ruler of the next World Empire. Verse 15 indicates that any person who does not bow to this image will be killed on the spot. So if you don't want to bow I suggest that you at least duck.

Revelation 13:16 And he causeth all, both small and great, rich and poor, free and bond, to receive a mark in their right hand, or in their foreheads: 17 And that no man might buy or sell, save he that had the mark, or the name of the beast, or the number of his name. 18 Here is wisdom. Let him that hath understanding count the number of the beast: for it is the number of a man; and his number is Six hundred threescore and six.

It's time for a quiz. What is the mark of the beast? I will give you a clue. A mark is simply some sort of identifying insignia. We are halfway there. Now it's your turn. What is a beast? I am certain that you remember that a beast represents a large government like a nation or empire. In this case the mark of the beast is an identifying emblem of the next World Empire. In Revelation 13:16 above, the Greek word translated "in" should probable rather be translated as "on". So this mark is probably something that a person wears. I think that the mark of the beast is an inscription worn on the hand or forehead. It could possibly even be an Islamic armband or headband that is already popular with every Islamist group from Libya to Afghanistan. By the way, I think that this mark is imposed upon the folks who live within the next World Empire and not upon the entire world. Please allow me to suggest that this mark may even primarily be imposed upon the citizens of Israel. Let's remember that this chapter was given to the Apostle John and largely concerns the nation of Israel during their time of Great Tribulation. For more about the "mark of the beast" please read my commentary titled "6 6 6 no microchip needed" in my book "Israel's Beacon of Hope".

We studied an entire chapter just so I could tell you about a talking hologram. The image of the beast is just a representation of a man. It is a symbol of the next World Empire or probably more specifically of its ruler. It will speak. It will probably even shoot lasers out of its eyes! Well it might not really shoot lasers. I made up that part on my own.

More from High Time to Awake

Available from Amazon.com, CreateSpace.com, and other retail outlets. Also available on Kindle and other devices.

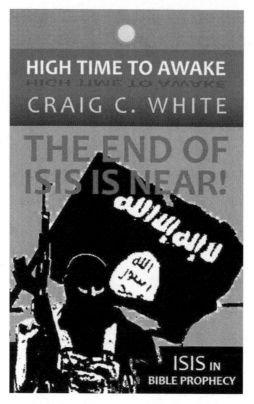

The End of ISIS is near thoroughly covers ISIS in bible prophecy. It also contains a collection of commentaries about present day prophecy whose subjects are current and widely varied.

What is really going on in the world? Will Al-Qaeda take Baghdad? Is all the fighting in the Middle East related? Why is Russia creating a Union? Has Egypt seen the last of the Muslim Brotherhood? What is the Pope up to? Will the Turkey-Israeli reconciliation agreement have a seven year term?

www.hightimetoawake.com

Chapter Ten

Revelation 13 Wounded

Image credit: Stephanie in love www.flickr.com/

You do that boo-boo that you do so well!

Revelation 13:1-3

By Craig C. White

In interpreting Revelation 13 there is a popular idea that the Antichrist will recover from a fatal head wound. Are we looking for a man who has been wounded yet lived? No. We are looking for an empire that has been wounded and lives again? We are looking for a revived gentile World Empire similar to the ancient Roman Empire or more likely the Turkish Ottoman Empire. Notice in the verse below that one of the beast's heads was wounded. Heads in this verse represent World Empires. Horns represent kings. The king isn't wounded. The empire is wounded and revives again. We are not looking for a man with a wounded head. We are looking for a revived gentile world empire!

Revelation 13:1-3 And I stood upon the sand of the sea, and saw a beast rise up out of the sea, having seven heads and ten horns, and upon his horns ten crowns, and upon his heads the name of blasphemy. 2 And the beast which I saw was like unto a leopard, and his feet were as *the feet* of a bear, and his mouth as the mouth of a lion: and the dragon gave him his power, and his seat, and great authority. 3 And I saw one of his heads as it were wounded to death; and his deadly wound was healed: and all the world wondered after the beast.

We are not looking for a wounded Antichrist. We are looking for a revived World Empire or a "New World Order". Unfortunately, the latter is a lot easier to find.

Chapter Eleven

Obama is supporting Erdogan

Photo credit: Ash Carter www.flickr.com DoD Photo by Glenn Fawcett (Released)

Erdogan is supporting the Muslim brotherhood

By Craig C. White

Saudi Arabia has accused US President Barack Obama of blocking heavy arms shipments from reaching the Kurds in Syria. These weapons are meant to help the Kurds to fight against ISIS. Since March 2015 Turkey and Saudi Arabia have been shipping an enormous stash of heavy weapons to Ankara Turkey's capital. Turkey would like to send these weapons to the *The Free Syrian Army* which consists not of Syrians but of Al-Qaeda rebels from Libya. The Free Syrian Army is the major force fighting against Syrian President Assad in Syria. The Free Syrian Army is fighting on behalf of the Muslim Brotherhood as well as on behalf of Turkish President Erdogan. The goal is to install Muslim Brotherhood leadership in Syria. Syria would then become the first nation to join Erdogan's revived Ottoman Empire.

Turkey recently deployed 54,000 troops on the Syrian border so I suspect that some of this weapons cache is meant to be used in a Turkish attack on Syria and on its capital city of Damascus.

Saudi Arabia wants some of these weapons to go to the Kurds fighting against ISIS in Syria. But Erdogan has announced that he wants to attack Damascus and also to stop the Kurds from creating a Kurdish state in Syria. So all of those weapons will be used or distributed by Erdogan as he sees fit. Erdogan wants to install Muslim Brotherhood leadership in Syria. The US is helping him to do that.

If you want to make sense of the US position in Syria and Iraq then you must realize that Obama is primarily supporting Erdogan. The US is supporting Turkey. That is a bad thing. Erdogan doesn't want ISIS or the Kurds to form a stronghold in Syria. If Erdogan were to attack ISIS he would not suffer politically but if he went to war with the Kurds he would enrage the large Kurdish population in Turkey. So Erdogan is preventing weapons supplied by Saudi Arabia from reaching the Kurds. If the Kurds don't have weapons then they will be easier to deal with once the Turkish Army enters Syria. US President Obama has been happy to assist Erdogan in his exploits.

This is all leading to the Turkish led destruction of Damascus predicted in Jeremiah chapter 49. Read my commentary titled "The nations are disquieted over Syria" in my book "Nation by Nation Verse by Verse".

Chapter Twelve

Intelligence reports reach Hamath

Turkey prepares to attack Damascus

By Craig C. White

In 2014 Turkey's parliament passed a mandate that allows the Turkish army to enter Syria over the next year. Turkish involvement in Syria has been protested by the Turkish people for the past few years. According to Jeremiah 49 Damascus will suffer attack and be destroyed.

Jeremiah 49:23 says that intelligence reports of the attack will come to Syria's northwestern cities. The attack emanates from Turkish border!

Jeremiah 49:23 Concerning Damascus. Hamath is confounded, and Arpad: for they have heard evil tidings: they are fainthearted; there is sorrow on the sea; it cannot be quiet.

Guess what? Syria's northwestern cities are hearing those intelligence reports now!

Starting in early September 2013 Turkey began moving heavy military equipment along Syria's northwestern border. Turkey's military equipment includes tanks, rocket-launchers, missile launchers, and anti-aircraft guns. Turkish military planes have also flown in to the region; those include F-16 fighters, tanker, and cargo planes.

We have been told that Syria may have used chemical weapons, and that justifies overthrowing the Syrian government. Don't be fooled. Whether or not Syria used chemical weapons; world powers will overthrow Syria. Jeremiah 49:25-27 tells us that Damascus will be besieged. The Syrians will not surrender; and all of the young men and Syrian army will be killed inside of the city.

I suspect that intelligence reports of a gathering attack will continue to increase. The next events that Jeremiah records are of terrified citizens in Damascus as they flee the city running for their lives. Damascus has a population of about 2.6 million in the metropolitan area. Hundreds of thousands of Damascus residents have already fled the city. Hundreds of thousands of Syrian refugees have also fled to Damascus from outlying areas. I suspect that the entire city will empty except for the young men and the Syrian Army (Jeremiah 49:26).

Chapter Thirteen

Aiming for Hamah

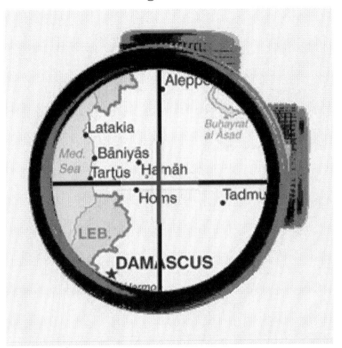

Copyright 2015 Craig C. White

Hamah will fall before Damascus

By Craig C. White

Things have changed in Syria. Huge arms shipments have upset the balance of power there. Beginning in March 2015 Turkey and Saudi Arabia have teamed up to flood Al-Qaeda rebels in Syria with heavy arms. The rebels are thrilled. They say that they are now able to conquer Syria's larger cities like Hamah, and Aleppo. Hamah is located about 70 miles from Turkey in western Syria. Hamah is mentioned in Jeremiah 49:23. In Jeremiah the cities of Hamah and Aleppo hears reports of a coming attack. Shortly afterwards Damascus is destroyed.

Jeremiah 49:23-25 Concerning Damascus. Hamath is confounded, and Arpad: for they have heard evil tidings: they are fainthearted; there is sorrow on the sea; it cannot be quiet. 24 Damascus is waxed feeble, and turneth herself to flee, and fear hath seized on her: anguish and sorrows have taken her, as a woman in travail. 25 How is the city of praise not left, the city of my joy!

Al-Qaeda rebels are fighting to take over Syria and to remove Syrian President Assad. The Free Syrian Army consists mostly of Al-Qaeda fighters from Libya. Al-Qaeda from northern Iraq (ISIS) as well as Al-Qaeda from Saudi Arabia is also fighting in Syria. These Al-Qaeda factions do not get along with one another. They are all fighting for their own preeminence over a vanquished Syria.

These huge arms shipments are being delivered mainly to the Free Syrian Army (or Al-Qaeda from Libya). These new weapons have already helped the rebels to launch a major attack on Aleppo, Syria's largest city. Al-Qaeda from Libya is fighting on behalf of the Muslim Brotherhood as well as on behalf of Turkish President Erdogan. The goal is to install Muslim Brotherhood leadership in Syria. Afterwards the plan is to take over the entire Middle East, central Asia and northern Africa. ISIS is the odd man out as far as Erdogan and the Muslim Brotherhood is concerned. That is because if ISIS (or Al-Qaeda from northern Iraq) conquers Syria then they would install their own leadership. The ISIS Caliphate is out. The Turkish Caliphate is in!

The heavily armed Free Syrian Army (Libya) is eager to strike Hamah. After they do then they will also strike Damascus. Will they do this alone? I think that the bible hints at a Turkish led attack on Damascus, Syria. Most of these weapons have been shipped directly to Turkey's capital city of Ankara. Ankara is located in the middle of Turkey far from the fighting in Syria.

In the bible the Antichrist is compared to the ancient Assyrian kings. In 734 BC the Assyrians attacked Syria and then attacked northern Israel. I think that Turkish President Erdogan will fulfill bible prophecy as he destroys Damascus and then leads the armies that are now fighting in Syria into northern Israel. Ezekiel chapter 38 describes this Turkish led invasion into Israel. Every nation that is listed in Ezekiel chapter 38 is fighting in Syria today!

The Al-Qaeda rebels are already attacking Aleppo. But I suspect that the big attack will come from the Turkish border. Be alert! Soon our news broadcasts will be filled with reports about an attack on the city of Hamah in Syria. Expect Damascus to fall next!

More from High Time to Awake

Available from Amazon.com, CreateSpace.com, and other retail outlets. Also available on Kindle and other devices.

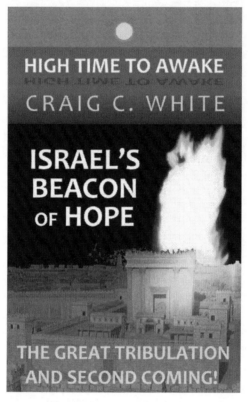

Israel's Beacon of Hope chronicles the trial of the nation of Israel during the Great Tribulation period. Happily it also explores the return of the Shekinah glory to Jerusalem, the return of all believing Jews throughout time to Israel, and life after the Tribulation. God's covenant with Israel is everlasting!

www.hightimetoawake.com

Chapter Fourteen

Hamah and Aleppo (and Arpad)

...will hear reports about a coming invasion.

By Craig C. White

The Prophet Jeremiah gives us a prediction about the destruction of Damascus, Syria. Along with Damascus, Jeremiah also mentions two other Syrian cities. They are Hamath and Arpad.

Jeremiah 49:23 Concerning Damascus. Hamath is confounded, and Arpad: for they have heard evil tidings: they are fainthearted; there is sorrow on the sea; it cannot be quiet.

In the verse above, Jeremiah mentions two cities; Hamath and Arpad. Both of these cities are located in northwestern Syria. Today Hamah is Syria's fourth largest city with a population of 313 thousand. Hamah is in the Hama Governorate of Syria. Hamah is south of Arpad but both cities are close to the Turkish border. Arpad is the modern day town of Tell Erfad (or Tell Rifaat) just to the north of Aleppo. Aleppo is Syria's largest city with a population of over 2.1 million. The city of Arpad is in the Aleppo Governorate of Syria.

What Jeremiah is trying to tell us is that the two large Syrian cities of Hamah and Aleppo along with the towns north of Aleppo will hear reports of a gathering invasion from the nearby Turkish border! Hamah and Aleppo's northern neighbors are fearful that they may be attacked.

Today Al-Qaeda rebels are assaulting Aleppo. Aleppo is Syria's largest city. Turkey is moving more heavy arms and troops to the Syrian border near Aleppo.

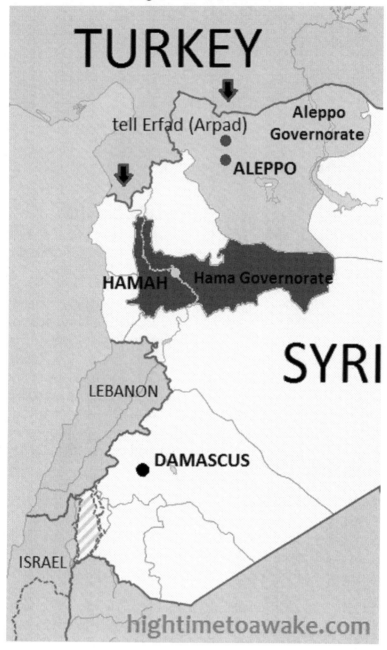

Hamah and Aleppo map: Notice the close proximity between two of Syria's largest cities and the Turkish border. Base map credit: NordNordWest

Hamah and Aleppo

...will hear reports about a coming invasion (Jeremiah 49:23).

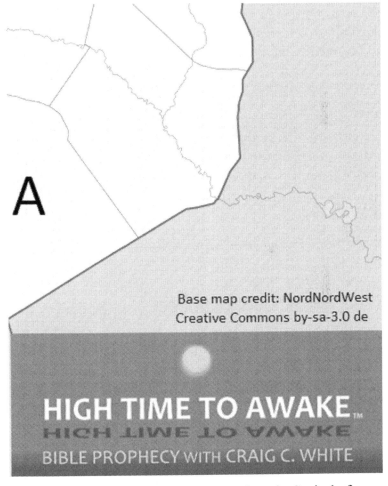

Base map credit: NordNordWest
Creative Commons by-sa-3.0 de

HIGH TIME TO AWAKE™

BIBLE PROPHECY WITH CRAIG C. WHITE

Turkish President Erdogan wants to invade Syria before a coalition government is formed in the Turkish Parliament. He considers that he will have less presidential authority after a coalition government is formed. This is very big

71

news. Erdogan has three goals. 1) To remove Assad from power. 2) To ensure that ISIS doesn't form a state in northern Syria. 3) To ensure that the Kurds don't gain too much control over a vanquished Syria. Erdogan's ultimate goal is to install Muslim Brotherhood leadership in Syria and then to form a four nation confederacy with Turkey, Syria, Iraq, and Iran. These nations will together conquer most of the Middle East!

Since March 2015 Turkey has been amassing enormous stockpiles of heavy weapons. These weapons were meant to be given to the Free Syrian Army fighting against Syrian President Assad. It seems that some of these weapons were also meant for the Turkish Army to use as they invade Syria.

Reports were leaked that the Free Syrian Army intended to use the weapons to attack Syria's larger cities like Hamah and Aleppo. As a matter of fact beginning in early July 2015 the Free Syrian Army launched their biggest attack yet on Aleppo.

Note: Don't let the name "Free Syrian Army" fool you. The Free Syrian Army was born in Libya and consists of Al-Qaeda soldiers from Libya. You won't find one single "Syrian" brigade among them.

The Free Syrian Army is fighting on behalf of the Muslim Brotherhood and also on behalf of Turkish President Erdogan. If the Free Syrian Army is able to take over Aleppo then the Turkish Army won't have to. But there is a problem. While Al-Qaeda from Libya (aka the Free Syrian Army) is attempting to overthrow Aleppo, ISIS has succeeded in gaining control of several towns just to the north of Aleppo. This is a problem for Turkish President Erdogan in two ways. First he doesn't want ISIS to create an Islamic State in Syria because Erdogan knows that whoever controls Syria also controls the new Islamic Caliphate. The other problem is that ISIS is taking control of the region between Turkey and Syria's larger cities. ISIS has cut off the supply route between Turkey and the Free Syrian Army fighting against Aleppo. Also ISIS is now blocking the route for a Turkish attack on Hamah, Aleppo, and most importantly Damascus!

Jeremiah identifies the town of Arpad located just to the north of Aleppo. Now that ISIS has taken control of Arpad and several other towns to the north of Aleppo, the Turkish Army will be forced to engage ISIS there before they can support or supply the Free Syrian Army in their fight against Aleppo. The Turkish Army will also be forced to deal with ISIS camped north of Aleppo before they can continue southwards towards Damascus. The presence of ISIS in the region north of Aleppo practically guarantees that the Turkish Army will have to enter Syria.

Well Turkey now has a stockpile of weapons and Turkish President Erdogan wants to invade Syria. Erdogan said that when he invades Syria he won't do it halfway. He will accomplish three main goals with overwhelming force. The ultimate goal is to remove Syrian President Assad from power in Damascus. Erdogan says that he will also prevent ISIS as well as the Kurds from establishing their own states inside of Syria.

The number one goal is the destruction of Syria's capital city of Damascus. Hamah and Arpad will hear reports of an invasion. These cities are along the path of an invasion launched from Turkey headed towards Damascus.

Jeremiah 49:24-25 Damascus is waxed feeble, and turneth herself to flee, and fear hath seized on her: anguish and sorrows have taken her, as a woman in travail. 25 How is the city of praise not left, the city of my joy!

The two Syrian cities of Hamah and Arpad will hear reports about a coming invasion. The inhabitants of Damascus will flee the city, and then Damascus will be destroyed.

Chapter Fifteen

Antichrist identified?!

Israel attack may follow Syria attack!

The Battles of Gog and Magog parallel the Assyrian led
Syria and Israel attacks of 734 BC and 701 BC.

By Craig C. White

I know that the names "Gog and Magog" sound strange to
many ears. But these two names are becoming a profound
part of the modern day fulfillment of bible prophecy. There
is much debate about who Gog and Magog are. First off,
Magog was a man. His name can be found in the
genealogies in Genesis 10:1-3 and 1Chronicles 1:5-6.
Magog was the son of Japheth the son of Noah. After
Noah's flood, Magog and his brothers settled modern day
Turkey. Gog is simply the name of the land that Magog
settled. For more commentary about Magog, his brothers,
and their land please read my commentary titled "Magog
Made Easy" in my book "Turkey invades Israel – Halfway
to Armageddon".

Ezekiel chapters 38 and 39 describe an attack into Israel led
by the primary leader (chief prince) of Turkey. This attack
is commonly called the battle of "Gog and Magog". I think
that Ezekiel chapter 38 describes a separate attack than
does Ezekiel chapter 39. I think that the Ezekiel 38 attack
will happen very soon. It will be led by Turkey after the
destruction of Damascus, Syria.

Ezekiel chapter 39 describes another battle that is also
described in Revelation 16:12 – 21 and Rev 19:17-18. This
battle is commonly known as the battle of Armageddon.
According to Ezekiel 39, the second battle of Gog and
Magog (or the battle of Armageddon) will happen a few
years after the first battle at the end of Israel's seven year
"Tribulation" period, and will also be led by the primary
leader of Turkey. Remember that Magog was the

prominent prince among his brothers. In bible prophecy Magog represents the primary leader of Turkey. During these battles "Magog" may not always be the same person, but he will always be the primary leader of Turkey. Now, if somebody asks you who Magog is; you can answer them directly, "Magog is the primary leader of Turkey". Today the Prime Minister of Turkey is Recep Tayyip Erdogan. He is antagonistic towards Israel and a prime candidate for our modern day "Magog". For a comparison between Ezekiel chapter 38 and Ezekiel chapter 39 please read my commentary titled "Magog Made Easier" in my book "Turkey invades Israel – Halfway to Armageddon".

In bible prophecy, the future Turkish led battles of "Gog and Magog" seem to correlate to the past Assyrian led attacks into Syria and Israel. The Assyrian led attacks happened in two parts. The first phase happened in 734 BC and the second phase in 701 BC. The first phase began with an invasion into Syria, and then a southward turn into northern Israel. At that time Israel was divided into two separate kingdoms. The northern kingdom headquartered in Samaria, and the southern kingdom headquartered in Jerusalem. The tribe of *Ephraim* refers to the northern kingdom of Israel. The attack into northern Israel was led by the Assyrian king named Tiglath-pileser (2Ki 12:18 – 18:16, 1Ch 5:26, Isa 66:19, Hos 5:13 – 10:6, Amos 1:3-5). Assyrian King Tiglath-pileser is also known as "Pul" in the King James Bible. The southern kingdom of the tribe of *Judah* was spared during the first phase of the Assyrian invasion. The second round of the Assyrian invasions was led by the then Assyrian king named Sennacherib. The second phase of the Assyrian invasion reached into the southern part of Israel near Jerusalem.

Like the Assyrian invasions of old, the future invasions described in Ezekiel chapters 38 and 39 will happen in two phases. Both battles will be instigated by the same nation; namely, Turkey. The first phase of the Turkish battles may begin with an attack into Syria just like the first round of the Assyrian invasion in 734 BC. So it would seem that the destruction of Damascus as prophesied in Isaiah 17 and Jeremiah 49 24-27 may be closely associated with the Magog led attack that is prophesied in Ezekiel 38. This sheds a great deal of light on current events and persons, as well as our position in the end time timeline. OK, now is the time to exercise some generosity. Give a poor guy some benefit. This is an astounding overview of prophetic events! As Christians, we should all be shouting this to every pastor and believer that we encounter. This is front page news! The city of Damascus is on the verge of destruction. All of the nations that will attack Israel as represented in Ezekiel 38:5 are now fighting in Syria. The Turkish army is amassed on the Syrian border. After the destruction of Damascus, the Turkish army may very well lead the armies of Iran, Sudan, and Libya in an invasion into Israel. Like I said, all of these armies are fighting in Syria today!

If we follow the Assyrian model then the invasion described in Ezekiel chapter 38 may extend only into northern Israel. The invasion described in Ezekiel chapter 39 will most certainly be accompanied by battles on every front throughout the entire land of Israel, including Jerusalem.

Isaiah 17:12-14 below also describes a multi-nation invasion into Israel.

Isa 17:12-14 Woe to the multitude of many people, *which* make a noise like the noise of the seas; and to the rushing of nations, *that* make a rushing like the rushing of mighty waters!13 The nations shall rush like the rushing of many waters: but *God* shall rebuke them, and they shall flee far off, and shall be chased as the chaff of the mountains before the wind, and like a rolling thing before the whirlwind.14 And behold at eveningtide trouble; *and* before the morning he *is* not.

This *is* the portion of them that spoil us, and the lot of them that rob us.

These verses refer to an event that happened around 701 BC. Assyria's king Sennacherib was in position to attack the city of Jerusalem. Overnight, God wiped out his army while they slept. Isaiah 37:6 below describes God's intervention.

Isa 37:36 Then the angel of the LORD went forth, and smote in the camp of the Assyrians a hundred and fourscore and five thousand: and when they arose early in the morning, behold, they *were* all dead corpses.

Isaiah 17:12-14 above contains similar language to that used in Ezekiel 38. It may be that these verses also implicate the near time Turkish led invasion into Israel. These same verses also sound similar to the swift destruction of Israel's enemies in the day of the Lord's vengeance at the end of Israel's seven year "Tribulation" period.

News Flash: The end time invader of Israel is called *the Assyrian* in Isaiah 10 and several other passages. Just as the Assyrian Kings invaded Syria and then Israel on two occasions, Magog will do the same. This invader is the same person that we call the *Antichrist*. The Antichrist is also called a *little horn* in Daniel 7 and 8. A little horn is a term used to describe a prince. Magog is described *as the chief prince of Meshech and Tubal* in Ezekiel 38:3. So the primary prince of Turkey is the Antichrist. It seems to me that we are very close to identifying the Antichrist as being Turkish Prime Minister Recep Tayyip Erdogan. God will use him to exercise his anger upon the nation of Israel, and Jesus Christ will destroy him at his coming.

Isa 10:5-6 O Assyrian, the rod of mine anger, and the staff in their hand is mine indignation. 6 I will send him against an hypocritical nation, and against the people of my wrath will I give him a charge, to take the spoil, and

to take the prey, and to tread them down like the mire of the streets.

The *hypocritical nation* described in the verses above is Israel. Yes this happened once before, but if you read the rest of Isaiah chapter 10 and the beginning of chapter 11 you will discover that this passage ends with the returning of the *Holy One of Israel* and a returning of the people of Israel to him. So the Assyrian is yet to come.

I believe that 2Thesalonians tells us that the reveling of the Antichrist on earth is the sign of the Rapture of the Church (please read my book "The Fall of Satan and Rise of the Antichrist"). If we are close enough to these events that we are able to identify the key players, then the Rapture of Church and the Tribulation period on earth must be very close indeed. It is High Time to Awake and tell your pastor!

More from High Time to Awake

Available from Amazon.com, CreateSpace.com, and other retail outlets. Also available on Kindle and other devices.

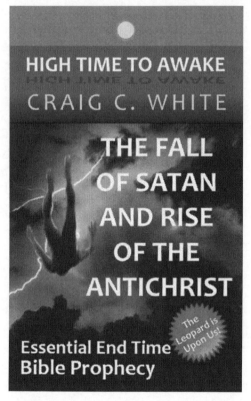

The Fall of Satan and Rise of the Antichrist explains how the Antichrist is the sign of the Rapture. This book contains "The Leopard is Upon Us!" about the formation of the final gentile world empire. It also looks at Mystery Babylon from a fly's eye view.

www.hightimetoawake.com

Chapter Sixteen

SPOILER ALERT! Erdogan is the Antichrist!

By Craig C. White

In Ezekiel 38:13 the United Arab Emirates, Saudi Arabia, and Lebanon all identify a Turkish ruler as the Antichrist! Or as the bible puts it; Sheba, Dedan, and the merchants of Tarshish all identify Magog as being the Assyrian!

Grab your thinking caps kids. This is going to get thick! In Ezekiel chapter 38 Turkey invades Israel. Three nations ask the invaders "Have you come to rob Israel?" The identity of these nations has long been debated. I am going to tell you who they are but this commentary isn't about their identity. It is about the question they ask and who it identifies.

In the verse below, three nations ask the ruler of Turkey "Art thou come to take a spoil?" That means "Have you come to plunder Israel?"

Ezekiel 38:13 Sheba, and Dedan, and the merchants of Tarshish, with all the young lions thereof, shall say unto thee, Art thou come to take a spoil? hast thou gathered thy company to take a prey? to carry away silver and gold, to take away cattle and goods, to take a great spoil?

These three nations are listed as Sheba, Dedan, and the merchants of Tarshish.

Sheba and Dedan were brothers (Gen 25:3). Sheba and Dedan come from Arabia. You have probably heard of the Queen of Sheba. The Queen of Sheba came from southern Arabia or what we know today as the United Arab Emirates (UAE), Oman, and Yemen. Dedan settled in northern Arabia or what we know today as Saudi Arabia. Two nations identified one to go!

Now let's identify the merchants of Tarshish. Tarshish is the rock island fortress off of the coast of the ancient city of Tyre. Jonah fled there when he tried to hide from God. The city of Tyre is in southern Lebanon. Tyre is called Sur today. The name Tyre and the name Sur mean *rock*. The merchants of Tarshish are from Lebanon. For a full exploration of Tyre along with its rock island fortress named Tarshish please read my commentary titled "Who were the Merchants of Tarshish?" in my book "Turkey invades Israel – Halfway to Armageddon".

Like I said before, this commentary is not about the identity of these nations. This commentary is about the question they ask. These nations ask "Have you come to plunder Israel?" or "Are you here to take a spoil?"

The word *spoil* or the term *to take a spoil* is used a lot in the bible. To take a spoil means that you take your enemy's possessions after you have conquered him. The bible records the actions of many nations as they spoil their defeated foes. In the bible Israel spoils several nations and several nations also spoil Israel.

Now here is the spoiler alert! When it comes to spoiling Israel; this is the end time action of the man we call the Antichrist! The Antichrist will invade Israel and rob them of their possessions. The Antichrist will spoil Israel!

There are several prophecies about the spoiling of Israel. Most of these prophecies have already been fulfilled by the Assyrian Empire, the Babylonian Empire, the Grecian Empire, and the Roman Empire. But most of these prophecies also refer to yet another end time invasion into Israel conducted by the next World Empire and led by the Antichrist.

When our three nations ask the Turkish ruler "Have you come to take a spoil?" they are recognizing bible prophecy written about the end time spoiler of Israel. In simple terms, the United Arab Emirates, Saudi Arabia, and Lebanon are recognizing this Turkish ruler as being the Antichrist! Today Turkish President Erdogan fills that role.

Here are some important verses about the end time spoiler of Israel. In the following verse the hypocritical nation is Israel. The Prophet Isaiah predicts the Assyrian invasion into Israel led by the Assyrian King Sennacherib in 701 BC. Isaiah also predicts the future invasion of Israel by the coming Antichrist. Notice that he will take a spoil!

Isaiah 10:6 I will send him against an hypocritical nation, and against the people of my wrath will I give him a charge, to take the spoil, and to take the prey, and to tread them down like the mire of the streets.

The Prophet Daniel also predicts the spoiling of Israel. This prophecy was already fulfilled by Antiochus Epiphanes in 167 BC. Antiochus Epiphanes represented part of the Grecian Empire. The verse below also predicts the exploits of the coming Antichrist.

Daniel 11:24 He shall enter peaceably even upon the fattest places of the province; and he shall do that which his fathers have not done, nor his fathers' fathers; he shall scatter among them the prey, and spoil, and riches: yea, and he shall forecast his devices against the strong holds, even for a time.

In the future a Turkish ruler will lead an invasion into Israel. Three nations will declare that he is the end time conqueror of Israel spoken about in the bible. They will ask "Have you come to conquer and then to plunder Israel?" "Have you come to take a spoil?" By asking this question they are identifying the Turkish ruler as the Antichrist.

The United Arab Emirates, Saudi Arabia, and Lebanon all understand bible prophecy. They all recognize that the future Turkish ruler is the person who the prophets have predicted would spoil Israel. They all recognize that Turkish President Erdogan is the Antichrist. So should we!

Chapter Seventeen

Elkosh O'gosh!

God the ensnarer

By Craig C. White

When Hebrew prophets talk about the burden of a city or nation they are describing the portion of God's judgment that it must endure. The book of Nahum is describing Nineveh's plight. In 612 BC God sent a flood of water to destroy Nineveh. I think that Nahum is also describing the plight of ISIS in Mosul today!

Nahum 1:1 The burden of Nineveh. The book of the vision of Nahum the Elkoshite.

The name Nahum means comfort. He didn't comfort the city of Nineveh but he did comfort the nation of Israel by telling them that one of their enemies would be vanquished by God. Nahum was one of the Israeli captives that were taken away by the Assyrian Empire around 740 BC. So during the time that Nahum wrote his book he lived in Assyria or what we call northern Iraq today. Nahum lived in a town called Elkosh. Today the small town of Elkosh is known as Alqosh. Alqosh is located about twenty miles to the north of the city of Mosul. As a matter of fact Alqosh overlooks the Mosul dam. If the Mosul dam was ever to burst, Alqosh is as close as you could get to the dam without drowning. What does the name Elkosh mean? Elkosh means God the ensnarer.

To ensnare means to catch something in a trap. God set a trap for Nineveh. God ensnared the city of Nineveh by planting it by the Tigris River. In 612 BC God sent a torrential rain which overflowed the banks of the Tigris River flooding the city. Today the city of Mosul is sitting in an even worse trap. In 1985 construction of the Mosul dam was completed. Ever since the dam was put into service there have been concerns about its stability and safety. It seems that the ground it was built on is dissolving! The dam requires constant upkeep to prevent it from failing. The Mosul dam is located just north of the city. If the dam burst it would send a sixty foot high wave of water over the city of Mosul. So Nahum the comforter represents God the ensnarer; otherwise known as Elkosh!

Chapter Eighteen

Mosul weather forecast

Rain in a dry place

By Craig C. White

Everybody likes to check the weather report occasionally. I suppose that even an ISIS rebel wants to know what the day will be like as he threatens the local populous. ISIS is headquartered in the city of Mosul in northern Iraq. Here is an actual Mosul weather forecast.

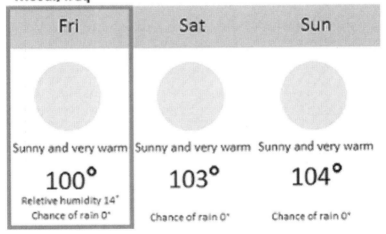

Copyright 2015 Craig C. White

It is summer in Mosul and as you can see the forecast is sunny and hot. There isn't any rain in the forecast at all. As a matter of fact there isn't even any moisture in the air. The relative humidity is often below 10%. That is extremely dry! This is a typical forecast for Mosul during the summer months. During the summer the chance of rain is 0% in Mosul.

Wouldn't it be nice if God sent just a little bit of rain to fall on ISIS to help curtail their wicked activities? What's that you say? Are you telling me that you don't believe that God controls the weather? Well one hot dry day long ago in the same place where Mosul sits today God did control the weather. On a day when there shouldn't have been any rain at all. In a place where it never rains; God sent rain!

Today Mosul sits on the Tigris River in the same place that the ancient city of Nineveh sat. In 612 BC God sent a torrential downpour upon the city of Nineveh. The rain overflowed the banks of the Tigris River flooding the city. The city was then ransacked by its enemies.

Nahum 1:8 But with an overrunning flood he will make an utter end of the place thereof, and darkness shall pursue his enemies.

The Prophet Nahum foretold the flooding of Nineveh. Nahum may also have predicted the future flooding of Mosul! Today the Mosul Dam is in danger of failing. If the dam burst then Mosul would be covered by sixty feet of water. Perhaps God will send another torrential rain to destroy ISIS in Mosul. Perhaps God will once again make it rain in a dry place just so we all know for certain that he did it!

Chapter Nineteen

ISIS just 10 miles from Nahum tomb!

Assyrian Christian family stands guard

By Craig C. White

ISIS has destroyed many historical sites in their conquest of northern Iraq and Syria. ISIS is now only 10 miles away from Nahum the prophet's tomb in the town of Alqosh near Mosul in northern Iraq. The family of an Assyrian Christian named Asir Salaam Shajaa have protected the Nahum tomb for generations.

I am certain that Nahum is buried in his home town of Alqosh in northern Iraq. He was part of the Israeli captives that were taken prisoner by the Assyrian Empire. Nahum foretold the destruction of the Assyrian Empire's capital city of Nineveh by a flood. Today the northern Iraqi city of Mosul is built around the ruins of Nineveh. Nahum may also predict the flooding of Mosul. The book of Nahum is short, only three chapters long. It may seem like a small thing to most of the world but now is the right time to remember Nahum. His prophecies may be completed in our time. The town of Alqosh overlooks the Mosul dam and is slightly elevated. It is as close to the dam as you can get without being drown in case the dam burst. Perhaps God will open the Mosul dam before ISIS destroys Nahum's grave.

More from High Time to Awake

Available from Amazon.com, CreateSpace.com, and other retail outlets. Also available on Kindle and other devices.

God's Great Expectations is about God's desire to know us, and about the ramifications of knowing him or rejecting him. It will challenge and inform every Christian. It answers the question "who can be saved?" It also contains an in-depth definition of hell in the bible, and a map of heaven! In "God's Great Expectations" I cover Jesus' claims to be God, as well as the Rapture of the Church.

www.hightimetoawake.com

Chapter Twenty

Revealing the Antichrist & False Prophet

Copyright 2015 Craig C. White

Gulen threatens Erdogan

By Craig C. White

We are in the midst of an end time scenario in every way possible. I think that 2Thesalonians 2:1-17 tells us that the revealing of the Antichrist is the sign of the Tribulation and quite possibly is also the sign of the Rapture. I also think that Ezekiel chapter 39 tells us that the Antichrist will be a Turkish Prime Minister or "primary governor" of Turkey. The man called *Magog* in Ezekiel chapter 38 is also a Turkish Prime Minister. Turkish ex-Prime Minister Erdogan is definitely Magog of Ezekiel chapter 38. He will invade Syria and then invade Israel soon. The Antichrist will be revealed with blasphemy, false wonders, and a seven year peace agreement concerning Israel. Turkish President Erdogan has recently claimed that he is god, and has also performed false miracles. Erdogan has also fulfilled several other bible prophecies that identify him as the Antichrist. So I am convinced that Erdogan is in fact the Antichrist.

There remains a serious threat to Erdogan's power. His name is Fethullah Gulen. Fethullah Gulen is an unconventional Muslim cleric who heads a wealthy religious/educational/business/political organization all about Islamic indoctrination and world supremacy. His Hizmet (meaning *service*) movement has been working subversively in Turkey for years to infiltrate the courts, police, and Turkish politicians.

Fethullah Gulen is above all a Muslim cleric. He teaches a brand of Islam that is inclusive of other religions. He is a smooth talker but he is an Islamist at heart. Gulen is a billionaire business man. Fethullah Gulen also operates over 1000 schools around the world. There are 300 Gulen sponsored schools in Turkey. The Turkish court just stopped Erdogan from closing them. Gulen runs the largest charter school organization in the US with over 140 grade schools and prep schools. His grade schools and high schools teach that Islam must dominate the world. His schools also prepare young Muslim students to one day take positions as government officials. Fethullah Gulen has millions of followers all over the world.

Even though Gulen and Erdogan were once allies, over the past fifteen years they have become arch rivals. Turkish Prime Minister Erdogan has accused Fethullah Gulen of operating a parallel government inside of Turkey. Fethullah Gulen has been accused of being behind a corruption investigation of several of Erdogan's political allies including Erdogan's son. It seems that Gulen sprang his political trap on Prime Minister Erdogan in 2013.

On December 17th 2013 the Turkish police arrested several sons of Turkish government officials. They also raided several Turkish banks. It seems that the police may have acted under the direction of Fethullah Gulen. Prime

Minister Erdogan accused Gulen of using police power to hold the Turkish government and financial institutions hostage! Erdogan issued an arrest warrant for Fethullah Gulen for undermining the Turkish government.

Fethullah Gulen has been accused of doing all of this even though he was forced to leave Turkey over fifteen years ago. Since 1999 Muslim cleric Fethullah Gulen has been living in the United States in Pennsylvania. Gulen lives in a palatial mansion under CIA protection.

Even though Fethullah Gulen now lives in Pennsylvania he still has a large number of his own operatives in the Turkish government. Gulen is also very popular with the Turkish people. A substantial percentage of Turks identify themselves as Gulenists.

Fethullah Gulen's greatest desire is to see Islam dominate the world. He employs an all-inclusive policy towards Christianity and other religions. The leadership of the Catholic Church praises him for his teaching on respecting other faiths. Gulen speaks in melodic tones and practices poetic phrases. In my opinion Fethullah Gulen sounds like a lamb but he actually speaks the words of a serpent. Gulen shows the hallmarks of the end time Antichrist or more likely the *False Prophet*. He is bent on world domination and has been working very subtly for years to build his power base. He is also a leading Muslim cleric, although he seems to have developed his own way of practicing Islam. Gulen is my new prime suspect for fulfilling the role of the False Prophet!

Check out Revelation 13:11 below. Most bible teachers see a false World Religion represented here. The false World Religion has two horns or rulers. It is my guess that one of these two rulers could be the Pope representing the Catholic Church as well as Protestants. The other ruler could be the False Prophet representing Islam.

Revelation 13:11 And I beheld another beast coming up out of the earth; and he had two horns like a lamb, and he spake as a dragon.

This false World Religion will be created after the next World Empire is formed. So we may not see the False Prophet officially take his position for a while. But I am certain that the world will be able to see him as he rises to power. Right now Fethullah Gulen is in a colossal power struggle with Turkish President Erdogan. The first step to Gulen's rise would be his reconciliation with Erdogan and his subsequent return to Turkey. I am keeping my eye on Turkish Muslim Imam Fethullah Gulen.

One way or another we are all very near the time of the revealing of the Antichrist, the Tribulation on earth, and the Rapture of the Church.

Chapter Twenty One

Closing prep schools in Turkey

A new Christian/Islamic religion

By Craig C. White

Turkish Prime Minister Erdogan is attempting to close prep schools in Turkey that are run by his political rival Muslim cleric Fethullah Gulen. Why is he closing prep schools? They seem harmless enough. Gulen is Erdogan's chief political rival in Turkey. Gulen has millions of supporters. His schools are producing many more.

In July 2015 the Turkish court rejected Erdogan's case for closing Gulen schools.

Imam Fethullah Gulen operates grade schools and high schools all over the world that promote a new variety of Social/Scientific/Christian/Islamic religion that welcomes all. Does this sound interesting? Do you want to join? I think that most people in the world already follow this type of faith. Of course this religion is not truly Christian. But this is the World Religion that will rule alongside of the next World Empire.

The Antichrist is Turkish President Erdogan. Imam Fethullah Gulen is wrestling Erdogan for political control over Turkey. Gulen is the "False Prophet". The False Prophet will rule alongside of the Antichrist during the Tribulation.

The end time is at our door. Jesus Christ will come to gather his Church very soon. A seven year time of trouble is coming upon Israel. A three and one half year period of Great Tribulation will soon encompass Jerusalem. The day of the Lord's wrath will fall on the whole world.

Chapter Twenty Two

Turkey-Israeli reconciliation agreement

Will it have a seven year term?

By Craig C. White

The Turkey-Israeli reconciliation agreement mainly consists of a twenty-one million dollar reparation payment by Israel to Turkey for the deaths of nine pro-Palestinian activists aboard the Gaza-bound flotilla of ships in May 2010. It was thought that the flotilla may be carrying weapons slated for Hamas. Turkish Prime Minister Erdogan instigated the shipment as a means to incite Israel to an act of war. Along with the payment Turkish Prime Minister Erdogan has also demanded a formal apology.

After the incident the two countries closed each other's embassies. The reconciliation agreement also includes plans to reopen the embassies. The agreement would also allow Turkey to make limited shipments to Gaza.

Israel tentatively says that they are close to finalizing the agreement but no date has been set.

I don't see this agreement specifically described in bible prophecy unless of course it contains a seven year term. Then this agreement could very well be the seven year long treaty that many believe marks the beginning of the seven year Tribulation period.

Dan 9:27And he shall confirm the covenant with many for one week: and in the midst of the week he shall cause the sacrifice and the oblation to cease, and for the overspreading of abominations he shall make *it* **desolate, even until the consummation, and that determined shall be poured upon the desolate.**

Considering the current state of prophetic events such as the seemingly near assault on Damascus (Jer 49:23-27), Egyptian fighting Egyptian (Isaiah 19:2), and the current hard press for the Israeli-Palestinian "Two state solution"; the Turkey-Israeli reconciliation agreement is worth watching.

I'm not sure when the Turkey-Israeli reconciliation agreement will be finalized but it seems to me that the bible describes an event that would facilitate the necessity of a peace treaty between Turkey and Israel.

Ezekiel chapter 38 describes a Turkish led attack into Israel. God fights against these invaders with heavy rain, disease, and infighting. So this attack is not entirely successful. I think that this Turkish led invasion happens after Turkey destroys Damascus, Syria. Afterwards Turkey and Israel would most certainly need to make peace!

Chapter Twenty Three

Obadiah

The garden tomb of Petra in the land of Edom image credit:
Arabian monkey www.flickr.com/

If you can't beat'em Edom!

By Craig C. White

Obadiah was a Hebrew prophet. He was part of the Jews who were taken captive by the Assyrian Empire. Obadiah probably lived in Assyria or today's northern Iraq. Obadiah gave his prophecy around 600 BC just after the fall of Jerusalem and Judea to the Babylonians. Obadiah wrote about God's judgement towards Edom which is in today's Jordan.

Oba 1:3-4 The pride of thine heart hath deceived thee, thou that dwellest in the clefts of the rock, whose habitation is high; that saith in his heart, Who shall bring me down to the ground? 4 Though thou exalt thyself as the eagle, and though thou set thy nest among

the stars, thence will I bring thee down, saith the LORD.

Edom is the mountainous region in southwestern Jordan today. Jacob's brother Esau settled in Edom. Edom was never a significant people group. The small population survived by controlling trade routes through the mountains.

Oba 1:2 Behold, I have made thee small among the heathen: thou art greatly despised.

The people of Edom won't play a part in end time events but the place will. In Obadiah God said that he would completely eradicate the family of Jacob's brother Esau along with his land Edom. Edom had participated in the ransacking of Jerusalem and the region of Judea by the Babylonians around 605 BC.

Oba 1:10 For thy violence against thy brother Jacob shame shall cover thee, and thou shalt be cut off for ever.

Edom also denied the people of Israel passage through the mountains during Israel's Exodus out of Egypt. That meant that the Jewish refugees had to go all the way around to the east side of Edom through the harsh desert. Shortly after the Babylonians conquered Jerusalem, the people of Edom began to move northward. During this period Edom was attacked by nomadic tribes. By 312 BC the Nabataeans drove them from the rock city of Petra. The Edomites were forced to move westward into the desert mountain region of southern Israel just south of the Dead Sea. That region became known as Idumea which means "pertaining to Edom". Today almost nobody lives in the land of Edom in Jordan. Today you will not find a people group or even a person that can trace their ancestry back to Edom or back to Jacob's brother Esau.

Oba 1:18 And the house of Jacob shall be a fire, and the house of Joseph a flame, and the house of Esau for

stubble, and they shall kindle in them, and devour them; and there shall not be any remaining of the house of Esau; for the LORD hath spoken it.

Judea is the region around Jerusalem in the southern half of Israel. People living in Judea are instructed to flee into Jordan when they see the Antichrist enter Jerusalem.

Mar 13:14 But when ye shall see the abomination of desolation, spoken of by Daniel the prophet, standing where it ought not, (let him that readeth understand,) then let them that be in Judaea flee to the mountains:

The Judean refugees will live in the region of Moab in Jordan for three and one half years. At the end of that three and one half year period the nation of Jordan will turn against them. The following verse describes Jesus as he travels through Edom towards Moab. He is fighting against the armies that have gathered to wipe out the Judean refugees now living in Jordan. Please read my commentary titled "Psalm 83 War" in my book "Israel's Beacon of Hope".

Isa 63:1-4 Who is this that cometh from Edom, with dyed garments from Bozrah?

While you have my book "Israel's Beacon of Hope" open also read my commentary "Revelation Wrath Path". It even has a map!

Note: Most Christians like to think that the Judean refugees will go to the rock city of Petra in the region of Edom. That is incorrect. God instructed Moab to receive his outcast people. Moab is the region just to the north of Edom in Jordan. There are already a lot of Syrian refugees living there today.

Isa 16:3-4 Take counsel, execute judgment; make thy shadow as the night in the midst of the noonday; hide the outcasts; bewray not him that wandereth. 4 Let mine outcasts dwell with thee, Moab; be thou a covert

to them from the face of the spoiler: for the extortioner is at an end, the spoiler ceaseth, the oppressors are consumed out of the land.

Edom is no longer a people group. Today southern Jordan represents Edom. Jordan will harbor Jewish refugees for three and one half years; not in Edom but in Moab. At the end of that time the nation of Jordan will turn against them. Jesus will travel through Edom on his way to save the Judean refugees in Moab just to the north of Edom.

Chapter Twenty Four

Turkey Parliament election results

By Craig C. White

Turkish President Erdogan's AKP party comfortably won the Turkey parliament election with 41% of the vote. The Republican People's Party came in second with 25% of the vote. In 2011 the AKP party won 49% of the vote so they lost 8% on June 7th, 2015. Erdogan and the AKP party were hoping to win a two thirds (or 66%) majority so that they could vote to change their constitution to make Erdogan the dictator of Turkey. Winning a two thirds majority is a very difficult feat. I didn't think that the AKP party would accomplish that but Erdogan's party still won the highest percentage of the vote. Erdogan hasn't lost his position or power. He has just been forced to form a coalition party.

Erdogan now has the opportunity to reconcile with his arch rival Fethullah Gulen along with the major opposition party, the Republican People's Party. Forming a coalition with the Republican People's Party would give Erdogan his two thirds or 66% majority. By the way Fethullah Gulen may be the False Prophet.

More from High Time to Awake

Available from Amazon.com, CreateSpace.com, and other retail outlets. Also available on Kindle and other devices.

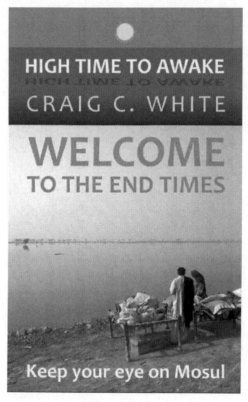

Welcome to the end times. You're late! Just to be certain that we are all aware; the Antichrist is now identifiable. The one sign that Jesus will give to Israel that proves he is truly their God is set to happen any day. Big trouble is about to come on earth. Jesus Christ is about to come with a trumpet call to raise the dead and to take away Christians. Jesus is coming. Not in five years but very very soon!

Welcome to the end times lists the biblical end times events that we can already see happening today!

www.hightimetoawake.com

Chapter Twenty Five

Will Erdogan reconcile with Gulen?

Is Fethullah Gulen the False Prophet?

By Craig C. White

Turkey held its parliamentary elections today (June 7, 2015). If Turkish President Erdogan's AKP party had won a two thirds majority of seats in the parliament then he could have changed Turkey's constitution and then voted himself as dictator of Turkey. Well Erdogan's party won only 41% of the votes. Not enough for a two thirds majority. But it isn't over yet! If Turkish President Erdogan is able to form a coalition majority party then he can still get his way.

Coming in second place was the Republican People's Party with 25% of the vote. If Erdogan is able to form a coalition government with the Republican People's Party then he would have his two thirds majority or 66%. The thing is the Republican People's Party is the major opposition party to President Erdogan and his AKP party. But let me warn you. I suspect that these two parties will unite to form a two thirds majority party in the Turkish Parliament.

Presenting Turkish Imam Fethullah Gulen. He is a powerful Muslim Cleric and Turkish President Erdogan's arch nemesis. Even though Fethullah Gulen was banished from Turkey by Erdogan in 1999, Gulen still has his own operatives well positioned inside of the Turkish government, courts, and police. As a matter of fact most people suspect that Fethullah Gulen is the power behind the Republican People's Party. So a deal with the Republican People's Party is also a deal with Fethullah Gulen.

Turkish President Erdogan is a dangerous man. He wants to conquer the Middle East and become the Sultan of a revived Turkish Empire. Fethullah Gulen is also a dangerous man. He is a Muslim cleric or Imam that teaches "understanding, respect, and interfaith tolerance". Sounds good right? Gulen isn't just a religious leader. He is a well-funded Islamist who also has a stated goal of world domination. Even though he now resides in Pennsylvania Fethullah Gulen is still the second most powerful figure in Turkish politics.

Turkish President Erdogan is proving himself as being the most likely candidate for being the Antichrist. It seems to me that a powerful Muslim religious leader that is so closely associated with President Erdogan is a very probable candidate to fulfill the role of the False Prophet spoken of in Revelation. The False Prophet performs miracles and causes unbelievers to worship the next World Empire (Rev 19:20). In Revelation 13 below I think that the two horned lamb represents a false World Religion that accompanies the next World Empire. This beast has two horns so the next World Religion may have two leaders. One of them is certainly the False Prophet.

Rev 13:11-12 And I beheld another beast coming up out of the earth; and he had two horns like a lamb, and he spake as a dragon. 12 And he exerciseth all the power of the first beast before him, and causeth the earth and them which dwell therein to worship the first beast, whose deadly wound was healed.

Will Erdogan reconcile with Gulen? Perhaps Erdogan and Gulen will conclude that by banding together they will be able to take over the Muslim world.

Consider this. Turkish President Erdogan and the Turkish army is about to enter Syria. He says that he intends to break up the Islamic State that has been formed by ISIS inside of Syria. More than anything Erdogan wants to remove Syrian President Assad from power in Damascus. When Turkey is able to conquer Syria and also defeat ISIS then Erdogan will become the new official ruler over the growing Islamic Caliphate! The Quran promises a future Islamic World Empire. Every Muslim is eagerly awaiting the ruler that is able to bring about the formation of this Caliphate. If Erdogan conquers Syria then afterwards Imam Fethullah Gulen will praise him as the promised Islamic Sultan! Together they will usher in the new Islamic Empire.

Keep your ears open. You may soon hear the name of Fethullah Gulen bouncing around your newscast like a ping pong ball.

Chapter Twenty Six

AKP and Republican People's Party
coalition a possibility

By Craig C. White

Last week Turkish President Erdogan's AKP Party won the parliamentary election with 41% of the vote. The Republican People's Party came in second with 25% of the vote. Erdogan was hoping to win 66% of the vote to give him a two thirds majority in the parliament. He would then be able to change the Turkish constitution to make himself the absolute authority in Turkey.

Now the AKP Party is forced to join together with another party to form a coalition party that together received more than 50% of the vote, or a simple majority.

One month after the Turkish parliamentary election President Erdogan and his AKP Party have not yet outlined their coalition party partners. President Erdogan finally asked the AKP party to form a coalition in mid-July. They have 45 days afterwards to form a coalition. If no coalition is formed then President Erdogan can call for a new election. The AKP Party has repeatedly said that they are willing to negotiate with any party.

The Republican People's Party is the major opposition party. Some in the party have said that they would prefer not to negotiate a coalition with the AKP Party. Former Republican People's Party leader, Deniz Baykal now Antalya deputy strongly argued that the Republican People's Party must negotiate with the AKP Party.

Last week nobody expected the possibility of an AKP Party and a Republican People's Party coalition. However I did suggest that it was a possibility. Now the AKP Party is hinting at a partnership with the Republican People's Party.

An AKP and Republican People's Party coalition would give Erdogan his 66% majority in the parliament.

Right now we are getting mixed messages from the Republican People's Party but the AKP Party insists that they are open to negotiate.

Muslim cleric Fethullah Gulen is suspected of being allied with the Republican People's Party. Gulen is Erdogan's chief rival for power in Turkish politics. Erdogan chased Gulen out of Turkey several years ago on treason charges. An AKP and Republican People's Party coalition would likely bring Gulen back into Turkey and back into power.

Turkish Imam Fethullah Gulen is one of the wealthiest and most influential men in the world. By the way, I think that Gulen is the False Prophet.

Chapter Twenty Seven

Gulen is the man of the hour

Fethullah Gulen Interview with Nuriye Akman in America
image credit: Diyar se www.flickr.com/

He may also be the False Prophet

By Craig C. White

Since the Turkish parliamentary elections everyone is talking about Imam Fethullah Gulen.

You may have never heard of Turkish Muslim cleric Fethullah Gulen but you had better start paying attention to him. Fethullah Gulen is much more than a cleric. He is a billionaire business man. He also operates schools all around the world that prepare young Muslims for political office. Gulen then helps his students to take government positions that serve his own plans. He preaches Islam in a soothing manner and has millions of followers in Turkey and millions more around the world. In 2013 Fethullah Gulen was named one of TIME magazine's World's 100 Most Influential People. Fethullah Gulen was also honored with the 2015 Gandhi King Ikeda Peace Award for his "global leadership toward reconciling differences". Past recipients include Nelson Mandela, Desmond Tutu, Michael Gorbachev, and Rosa Parks. The Catholic Church is also actively participating in Gulen's "Hizmet" movement that promotes interfaith relations.

Muslim cleric Fethullah Gulen is Turkish President Erdogan's arch rival. After the last Turkish elections Gulen company stocks soared in price while every other ranking stock on the Turkish market sank.

Fethullah Gulen is suspected to be the power behind the Republican People's Party which finished second behind Erogan's AKP party in the June 7, 2015 election. Erdogan chased Gulen out of Turkey in 1999. Now Erdogan may be forced to reconcile with Gulen in order to form a majority party.

Imam Fethullah Gulen preaches Islam packaged in a way that even the western world is buying. Fethullah Gulen is my top candidate for fulfilling the role of the False Prophet mentioned in Revelation.

Chapter Twenty Eight

Egypt's Evil President Morsi will be reinstated!

Photo credit: jay8085

Take a picture of the Pyramids. It will last longer!

By Craig C. White

Do you remember Egypt's terrible President Morsi? Mohamed Morsi was the Muslim Brotherhood candidate for president of Egypt. He was elected and became president of Egypt in June 2012. Morsi attempted to turn Egypt into a strict Islamist state. The Egyptian army removed Morsi from office in July 2013. Now Egypt has plans to execute Morsi. Well guess what? I think that evil President Morsi will return to power in Egypt!

According to Isaiah 19 Egypt will be led by a cruel leader. He will be in power before, during, and even after the seven year long Tribulation period.

Isaiah 19:4 And the Egyptians will I give over into the hand of a cruel lord; and a fierce king shall rule over them, saith the Lord, the LORD of hosts.

Isaiah 19:4 above identifies Egypt's terrible ruler in two different ways. He is called a *cruel lord* and he is also called a *fierce king*.

Since Isaiah gave Egypt's rotten ruler two separate titles I have wondered if this verse was identifying two separate persons or if it was identifying only one person but describing him in two separate ways. Just so you know. There is no punctuation in the original Hebrew language.

I think that Isaiah has described one person who will serve as Egypt's ruler on two separate occasions. President Morsi has already served as Egypt's ruler once but I think that he will serve once more as Egypt's *fierce king*.

The bible tells us that Egypt will be conquered by the coming Antichrist. The Antichrist and his armies will rob Egypt of its treasures.

Dan 11:42 He shall stretch forth his hand also upon the countries: and the land of Egypt shall not escape. 43 But he shall have power over the treasures of gold and of silver, and over all the precious things of Egypt: and the Libyans and the Ethiopians *shall be* at his steps.

In case you didn't already know, I think that the bible identifies a Turkish Prime Minister as the Antichrist. I think that that person is in fact newly elected President Erdogan who served as Prime Minister of Turkey for twelve years. President Erdogan is an ally of the Muslim Brotherhood just as is Mohamed Morsi.

During the first half of the Tribulation period Turkish President Erdogan will lead the Turkish army along with Al-Qaeda from Libya and Sudanese rebels into Egypt. Erdogan will conquer Egypt and install Muslim Brotherhood leadership there. Mohamed Morsi will once again serve as Egypt's terrible ruler!

Last week Muslim Brotherhood supported Al-Qaeda rebels from Libya together with Al-Qaeda rebels from northern Iraq (ISIS) conducted a major offensive on Egypt's Sphinx and Pyramids. According to these Islamist terrorists, anything that doesn't glorify their brand of Islam must be destroyed. Folks are now wondering if Egypt's historic treasures and landmarks could possibly one day be destroyed. One day soon Turkish President Erdogan will conquer Egypt and rob it of its treasure. Then under Egypt's reinstated fierce king Mohamed Morsi the Sphinx and the Pyramids will certainly be devastated.

Chapter Twenty Nine

Tribulation checklist

By Craig C. White

Guess what folks? I think that the Tribulation could begin as early as Sept. 13, 2015. I am sure? Nope. But I am sure that the following events lead up to the Tribulation. And I am certain that these events will happen soon! The thing about the Tribulation period is that Christians may be taken up to heaven before it begins! Please read my commentary titled "Jubilee September 26, 2022 date setting!" in my book "Welcome to the end times".

Here is a detailed explanation of each event. You will of the Tribulation checklist on the following pages.

✓ ISIS gains control of Kobani.

ISIS almost took over Kobani, Syria last year but Kurdish troops stopped them. Now the Kurdish troops have left Kobani and ISIS is on the way back there! The Prophet Nahum may make a minor reference to the conquering of Kobani by ISIS. ISIS will be in Mosul, Iraq celebrating the conquest of Kobani when the Mosul dam bursts! ISIS represents a renewed Assyrian State! Read my commentary titled "Will Mosul fall after Kobani?" in my book "The End of ISIS is near!".

✓ June 7, 2015 Turkey holds election. President Erdogan's AKP party wins most parliamentary seats.

The Turkish election is not mentioned in the bible but Turkish President Erdogan wants complete control over the Turkish government. If his AKP party wins a two thirds majority in the parliament then he will be able to do anything that he wants to. Erdogan is the Antichrist! Read my commentary titled "What is Erdogan up to?" in my book "Welcome to the end times".

hightimetoawake.com

HIGH TIME TO AWAKE.
BIBLE PROPHECY WITH CRAIG C. WHITE

Tribulation checklist
By Craig C. White

Guess what folks? I think that the Tribulation could begin as early as Sept. 13, 2015. I am sure? Nope. But I am sure that the following events lead up to the Tribulation. And I am certain that these events will happen soon! The thing about the Tribulation period is that Christians may be taken up to heaven before it begins!

✓ ISIS gains control of Kobani.

- ✓ June 7, 2015 Turkey holds election. President Erdogan's AKP party wins most pariamentary seats.

- ✓ ISIS flooded in Mosul.

- ✓ Turkey invades Syria, wipes out Damascus.

- ✓ Russia continues conquering nations along its western border beginning with Ukraine.

- ✓ Turkey leads the forces fighting in Syria into Israel.

- ✓ Signing of 7 year term Turkey/Israel reconciliation agreement.

- ✓ ***Tribulation begins***

✓ ***Tribulation begins***

✓ Turkey, Syria, Iraq, and Iran form the core of a new Islamic Union represented by a leopard.

Save this checklist and keep it handy. You can check off each event as it happens. If you are a Christian then you will see the day of your salvation drawing near. If you don't believe in Jesus Christ then you are about to suffer through the most terrible time of trouble that the earth has ever seen.

It's High Time to Awake!

✓ **ISIS flooded in Mosul.**

The Prophet Nahum is all about the destruction of the ancient Assyrian capital city of Nineveh. Today Mosul in northern Iraq is built around the ruins of ancient Nineveh. Things in Mosul look a lot like they did when Nineveh fell in 612 BC. Please read my commentary titled "The End of ISIS is near!" in my book "The End of ISIS is near!".

✓ **Turkey invades Syria, wipes out Damascus.**

In Jeremiah chapter 49 two northwestern Syrian cities hear of an invasion coming from Turkey. Those two cities are Hamah and Aleppo. Jeremiah chapter 49 along with Isaiah chapter 17 foretells the destruction of Damascus. Read my commentary titled "The nations are disquieted over Syria" in my book "Nation by Nation Verse by Verse".

✓ **Russia continues conquering nations along its western border beginning with Ukraine.**

Russia has already created a new Russian economic Union but they won't stop there. Daniel chapter 7 tells us that Russia will conquer several nations along its western border. Russia will form a new Russian Union. Please read my commentary titled "The Leopard is Upon US!" in my first book "The Fall of Satan and Rise of the Antichrist".

✓ **Turkey leads the forces fighting in Syria into Israel.**

Turkish President Erdogan is the "chief prince" or primary governor of Turkey mentioned in Ezekiel 38 and 39. He will lead two separate invasions into Israel. I think that the first attack will happen after the destruction of Damascus. The second attack is the battle of Armageddon. Please read my commentary titled "Magog Made Easy!" in my book "Turkey invades Israel – Halfway to Armageddon".

✓ **Signing of 7 year term Turkey/Israel reconciliation agreement.**

After Turkey invades Israel they will need to form a peace treaty. Most bible teachers see this treaty as the event that marks the beginning of the seven years long Tribulation period. I think that the Tribulation period may actually begin with the Turkish led invasion into Israel. Please read my commentary titled "Peace Peace" in my book "Bible Prophecy 2014-2015".

✓ ****** Tribulation begins! ******

121

The Tribulation was designed for Israel's chastisement. God will lead Israel back to himself through much suffering. During the Tribulation God will also judge the nations of the earth. There will be many wars and natural disasters. Many people will be killed and many will also die of starvation and disease. There will be multiple horrific earthquakes and tidal waves. The Tribulation will be so bad that God has provided a way to escape it through the Rapture. The Rapture is the taking away from earth all of the believers in Jesus Christ. The Rapture begins with the resurrection of the dead! Please read my commentary titled "Tribulation Timeline" in my book "Welcome to the end times".

✓ **Turkey, Syria, Iraq, and Iran form the core of a new Islamic Union represented by a leopard.**

There is a new world empire coming. It will be created when the European Union, the new Russian Union, and a new Middle Eastern Union combine under a ten king council. The Middle Eastern Islamic Union will be represented by a leopard. It will probably be formed after the Destruction of Damascus and after Turkey installs Muslim Brotherhood leadership there. I think that this will happen early on during the seven year Tribulation period. Please read my commentary titled "The Leopard is Upon US!" in my book "The Fall of Satan and Rise of the Antichrist".

Save this checklist and keep it handy. You can check off each event as it happens. If you are a Christian then you will see the day of your salvation drawing near. If you don't believe in Jesus Christ then you are about to suffer through the most terrible time of trouble that the earth has ever seen.

Chapter Thirty

WARNING TO JERUSALEM

Flee! Erdogan is coming!

By Craig C. White

Do you remember when Babylonian King Nebuchadnezzar invaded Jerusalem and destroyed the temple? He also took away Jewish captives. Do you remember when Grecian King Antiochus Epiphanes invaded Jerusalem and took one half of the people away? In both instances many Jews were killed. Well there is another invader on his way to Jerusalem. He is Turkish President Recep Tayyip Erdogan. President Erdogan is the Antichrist. He will be worse than any other invader before him.

Erdogan will attack Jerusalem and Judea. His army will break into your homes. He will take one half of the people captive. He will kill anybody trying to leave Jerusalem. If you are caught inside of Jerusalem when Erdogan arrives then the only way to escape is to wait on Mt. Zion. The bible warns the inhabitants of Judea to watch for this invasion and to flee to Moab of Jordan. Today we can see this invasion approaching.

Allow me to tell you what to watch for. Turkey will enter Syria from its northwestern border near Hamah. The Turkish army will fight against the Syrian National Guard and the Syrian Army in Damascus. Turkey will besiege Damascus until the last Syrian soldier is killed. The old city of Damascus will be left in ruins. Its inhabitants will flee to Kerak in Jordan. They will become refugees there.

Note: ISIS in Mosul may be flooded before Erdogan attacks Damascus. These things are likely to happen this year (2015).

From Damascus Erdogan will lead Al-Qaeda from Libya, Hezbollah from Iran, and Hezbollah trained rebels from

Sudan into northern Israel. All of these armies are fighting in Syria today! God will fight against these armies with a tremendous rainstorm, debilitating disease, and infighting. Perhaps after this invasion a seven year peace treaty will be signed between Erdogan and Israel. Erdogan will break this treaty in the middle of its term. This isn't the invasion that I am warning you about. This invasion takes place about three and one half years before the invasion into Jerusalem.

After Damascus is overthrown Erdogan will install new Muslim Brotherhood leadership in Syria. Once that is accomplished Turkey, Syria, Iraq, and Iran will form a confederacy along with four other nations or terrorist groups. This confederacy or Union will be represented by a leopard. This new Islamic Union will wage war on the rest of the Middle East, central Asia, and northern Africa. In northern Africa Al-Qaeda from Libya and Hezbollah trained fighters from Sudan will join the Turkish army. These will be the deadliest wars in history with about 400,000,000 killed. At first only Israel and Jordan will be spared. But then Erdogan will come away from conquering northern Africa including Egypt and enter into Jerusalem. The bible compares the coming Antichrist to Antiochus Epiphanes. Antiochus Epiphanes attacked Egypt more than once. Erdogan may also enter Egypt on more than one occasion. So don't let your guard down if Erdogan doesn't attack Jerusalem after his first visit into Egypt.

Attention inhabitants of Judea! This verse was written to YOU!

Mat 24:43 But know this, that if the goodman of the house had known in what watch the thief would come, he would have watched, and would not have suffered his house to be broken up.

All inhabitants of Judea please listen! You must watch.

Mat 24:15-18   When ye therefore shall see the abomination of desolation, spoken of by Daniel the

prophet, stand in the holy place, (whoso readeth, let him understand:) 16 Then let them which be in Judaea flee into the mountains: 17 Let him which is on the housetop not come down to take any thing out of his house: 18 Neither let him which is in the field return back to take his clothes.

You must flee to the Jordanian mountains when you see this invasion approaching. You will be taken care of in Jordan just like so many Syrian refugees are being cared for today. You will remain there for three and one half years. At the end Jordan, Lebanon, and northern Iraq will send armies to destroy you but your Messiah will return to fight against them.

When Erdogan invades Jerusalem it is the beginning of three and one half years of terrible persecution. At the end of this three and one half year time period the Messiah of Israel will return! After your Messiah rescues the Judean refugees in Jordan then he will deliver the few remaining Jews in Jerusalem.

Matthew 24:21 For then shall be great tribulation, such as was not since the beginning of the world to this time, no, nor ever shall be.

This is the time of Jacob's trouble.

Jeremiah 30:7 Alas! for that day is great, so that none is like it: it is even the time of Jacob's trouble; but he shall be saved out of it.

Turkish President Erdogan will come from invading northern Africa when he enters Jerusalem. The Judean residents are instructed to flee to the Jordanian wilderness. Anybody left in Jerusalem must remain on Mount Zion if they want to escape their enemies. Jerusalem, Judea, and all of Israel will suffer for three and one half years but at the end Jesus Christ will rescue them.

###

By the way, if you review this book on Amazon I will let you park in your pastors parking space next Sunday!

Thank you in advance, Craig C. White

About the Author

Craig C. White

Craig C. White was born in 1958 and born again in 1964. In the 1980's he was an active member of Calvary Church in Santa Ana, California. The expositional bible teaching of then pastor Dr. David Hocking played a major role in building Craig's biblical literacy. He has been a serious bible student ever since.

The views contained in my commentaries are solely my own. I do not accept other views just because they are popular. I try to understand what the bible says. You will find clear interpretations here that you will scarcely find elsewhere.

More from High Time to Awake

Available from Amazon.com, CreateSpace.com, and other retail outlets. Also available on Kindle and other devices.

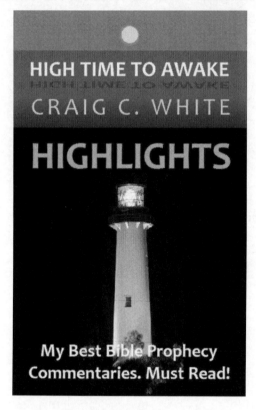

High Time to Awake **Highlights** contains a collection of my best bible prophecy commentaries. I chose these commentaries to be among my best based on their urgency of message, their timeliness, their carefulness of research, the attention given in writing them, their helpfulness to understanding end time prophecy, and also for the scarcity of these views being shared elsewhere. I hope these commentaries give you a solid foundation of understanding for our times, and also a clearer awareness of God's presence in your life.

www.hightimetoawake.com

Printed by Amazon Italia Logistica S.r.l.
Torrazza Piemonte (TO), Italy

52739524R00074